Contents

STRAND 1
Who am I?

STRAND 1
Who am I?

STRAND 2
Minding Myself and Others

STRAND 2
Minding Myself and Others

STRAND 3
Team Up

STRAND 4
Mental Health and Wellbeing

STRAND 3
Team Up

STRAND 3
Team Up

STRAND 3
Team Up

Preface

Welcome to *New Healthy Lifestyles*

This new edition retains all of the lessons required for teaching the existing modular course: simply follow the **Modular Course Overview** on page v to do so. It is also designed to fulfil the criteria for teaching SPHE as a **Short Course** for the new Junior Cycle: The contents list on page iii is structured around the topics and strands recommended for the new Short Course in SPHE.

The **Up for the Challenge** feature at the end of each topic allows students to apply what they have learned to real life situations. These challenges also prepare students for assessment related to the certification of the short course; see your **Teacher's Resource Book on gillmacmillan.ie** for more detail.

We have retained many of the favourite features of the highly popular first edition, such as crosswords and wordsearches. We have also added the following features, which means that, whatever approach your school is taking for SPHE, you will have an easy-to-follow and comprehensive set of lessons for your classes. These new features include:

- A ready-to-go, lesson-by-lesson approach
- A Teacher's Resource Book available on gillmacmillan.ie which gives practical guidelines on how to implement the material in the student books
- Links to websites which provide extra background information for the teacher and enhances the student's knowledge of a topic
- Each lesson is based on the experiential learning model which means that students will be actively engaged in their own learning
- Each lesson concludes with a **Learning Keepsake**, which ensures students maintain a personal learning journal as recommended by the NCCA.
- Exercises to improve students' literacy and numeracy skills are in-built
- An **eBook** version which contains many fun videos and animations to enhance lessons
- Extra lessons and exciting and interesting worksheets and articles in our Teacher's Resource Book.

New Healthy Lifestyles has received very positive reviews from SPHE teachers who have used it in class. They have found it fun, relevant and up to date and we hope you do too!

Edel O'Brien and Catherine Deegan

NEW

Healthy
Lifestyles 3

The Complete Package for Junior Cycle SPHE

Catherine Deegan & Edel O'Brien

GILL & MACMILLAN

Gill & Macmillan
Hume Avenue
Park West
Dublin 12
with associated companies throughout the world
www.gillmacmillan.ie

Design by Tanya M Ross Elementinc.ie
Illustrations by Derry Doyle

The paper used in this book is made from the wood pulp of managed forests. For every tree felled, at least one tree is planted, thereby renewing natural resources.

For permission to reproduce photographs, the authors and publisher gratefully acknowledge the following:

© Advertising Archives: 62, 97B; © Alamy: 64CT, 64T, 97CT, 97C, 117, 148, 158L, 180, 182L, 182R; © Getty Images: 49, 85, 184; © Rex Features/c.CW Network/ Everett: 97T; © Rex Features/Moviestore: 97TB; © Shutterstock: 1, 4, 7, 21, 28, 37, 39, 41, 60, 63, 64CL, 64CR, 68, 70, 73, 74, 88, 92, 95, 97CB, 97BT, 102, 107, 114, 122, 128, 133, 140, 144, 150, 157, 158R, 161, 169, 182C; Courtesy of Al-Anon/Alateen: 174; Courtesy of Aware: 174; Courtesy of BeLonG To: 137, 174; Courtesy of Bodywhys: 174; Courtesy of Cura: 174; Courtesy of Heads Up: 174; Courtesy of Rainbows Ireland: 174; Courtesy of the ISPCC: 174; Courtesy of safefood.eu: 64B; Courtesy of the Samaritans: 174; Courtesy of the Society of St Vincent de Paul: 174.

The authors and publisher have made every effort to trace all copyright holders, but if any has been inadvertently overlooked we would be pleased to make the necessary arrangement at the first opportunity.

Acknowledgements
The authors and publisher are grateful to the following for permission to reproduce copyrighted material:

The DETER strategy is used with permission of www.howtostudy.com
The FESTIVAL symptoms are used with permission of www.aware.ie
Physical Activity Guidelines are used with permission of www.getirelandactive.ie

The authors and publisher have made every effort to trace all copyright holders, but if any has been inadvertently overlooked we would be pleased to make the necessary arrangement at the first opportunity.

Modular Course Overview

My Rights and the Rights of Others

● Lesson 1 Work Contract

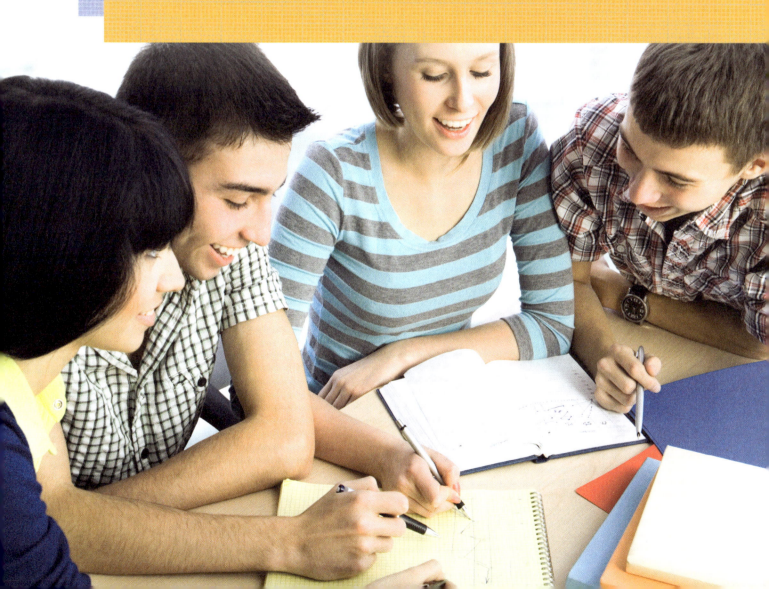

LESSON 1
Work Contract

At the end of this lesson . . .
. . . you will have drawn up the ground rules to facilitate a good learning environment.

Key Words
- Contract
- Learning environment

 # Keyskill
- Working with Others

Work *Contract*

First, let's review the ground rules that helped the SPHE class to work well last year and adjust the contract if necessary.

What helped the class run well?

_____

_____

_____

What kinds of behaviour are unhelpful in class?

_____

_____

_____

_____

What rules would you put in place to make sure that everyone works well in SPHE?

_____

_____

_____

_____

Group Activity

Discuss your ideas with the group.
Perhaps others in the group have similar or different views from you. Try to come to an agreement over the ground rules the group would like to implement. Write the agreed ground rules here.

_____

_____

_____

_____

Class Activity

Choose one person from your group to share your group's ideas with the rest of the class. The class as a whole must now try to agree on a set of guidelines. Remember: this includes the teacher too!

Once everyone has agreed on the guidelines, perhaps you could design a poster, banner or collage to hang on the classroom wall.

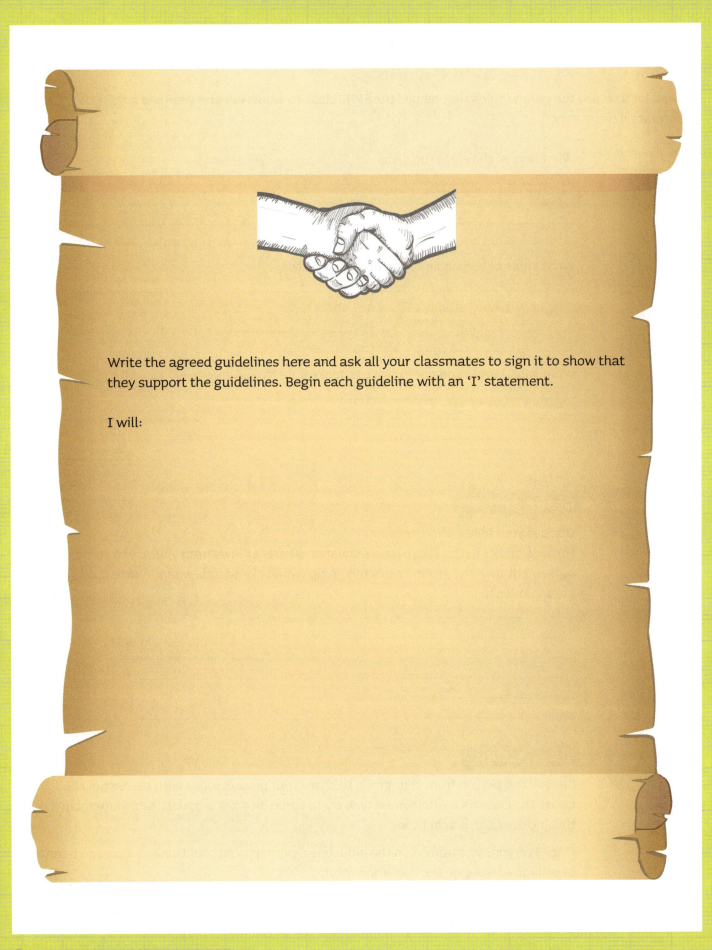

Write the agreed guidelines here and ask all your classmates to sign it to show that they support the guidelines. Begin each guideline with an 'I' statement.

I will:

Learning *Keepsake*

Three things I have learned about a good learning environment are:

1. _____

2. _____

3. _____

As a result of what I have learned about a good learning environment, I will:

_____

_____

_____

_____ has shared this Learning Keepsake with me _____

Name of student   Parent's/guardian's signature

Topic Review

Date / /

In this topic I learned about

_____

This topic is useful to me in my life because

_____

_____

In this topic I liked

_____

_____

In this topic I did not like

_____

_____

I would like to find out more about

_____

_____

Key Skills I have used in this topic are:

- ☐ Managing myself
- ☐ Staying well
- ☐ Communicating
- ☐ Being creative
- ☐ Working with others
- ☐ Managing information and thinking

*Are you up for the challenge?

Look up the equal status acts at culturewise.ie, and based on your research summarise the act and draw up an equality charter for your school.

Weblink

www.culturewise.ie/equal-check/pdf/the_equal_status_acts_2000_and_2004_1.pdf

TOPIC 2

Self Management

LESSON 2
Goal Setting for Third Year

At the end of this lesson . . .

. . . you will have set long-term and short-term goals for your Junior Certificate.

Key Words
- Goal
- Strategy

Keyskill
- Managing Myself

Looking *Forward*

Individual Activity

Write in the crystal ball the things you would like to achieve over the next year. You can include your family life, your friendships, your education and your hobbies – and any other aims.

Setting goals

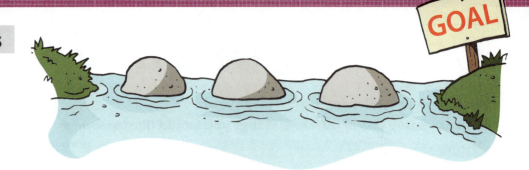

To make your hopes a reality, you need to set goals. Goals give you a sense of purpose and allow you to make a plan to achieve your targets. In order to achieve your long-term goals you need to set short-term goals, which are the stepping stones towards your long-term goals. For example, in third year a long-term goal might be to get a good result at Junior Cycle; and in order to achieve this your short-term goals could be to do well in class exams.

Individual Activity

Look at the calendar below.

1. In the box for September, write down your results from the summer exams. In the box for May, write down the results you hope to get in your Junior Cycle.

2. Write on the calendar any important assignments/projects/exams that you will have to complete. Include the specific dates if you know them.

3. Write in any other short-term goals you need to complete in order to achieve your long-term goals.

September	October	November	December	January

February	March	April	May Junior Cycle Exams	

Individual Activity

1. What type of goals did you include in your crystal ball?

    _____

    _____

2. How easy was it to identify your goals?

    _____

    _____

3. What goals are common to everyone in the class?

    _____

    _____

4. Do you think that having the same long-term goals as someone else means that your short-term goals will also be the same? Give reasons for your answer.

    _____

    _____

Get SMART

To achieve your short-term and long-term goals you need to have a strategy. One type of strategy is the SMART strategy, which states that goals should be:

- **Specific:** State exactly what you want to achieve. For example, 'I want to improve my maths grade by at least one grade.'
- **Measurable:** Record your improvements so that you can see your progress as you move towards your goal. 'I will work on my geometry and trigonometry.'
- **Achievable:** Break down your goal into achievable steps. 'I will answer the geometry and trigonometry questions in past exam papers.'
- **Realistic:** Set goals that you are able to accomplish. Don't try and do all the past papers at once; keep a checklist of the years you need to do and tick them off as you complete each paper.
- **Time-based:** How much time do you need to achieve your goal? Decide when you will start and when you will finish – and stick to it. Make sure to take into account all the other demands on your time when planning your goals.

Learning *Keepsake*

Three things I have learned about setting goals are:

1. _____
2. _____
3. _____

As a result of what I have learned about setting goals, I will:

_____
_____
_____

_____ has shared this Learning Keepsake with me _____
Name of student   Parent's/guardian's signature

LESSON 3
Organising My Time

At the end of this lesson . . .
. . . you will have reflected on how you spend your time each day
. . . and you will have drawn up a personal study timetable.

Key Word
- Commitments
- Timetable

 # Keyskill
- Managing Myself

Individual Activity

Look at the time management wheel. Taking the centre as 0 hours and the outer edge as 12 hours, fill in how much time you spend on each activity on an average day.

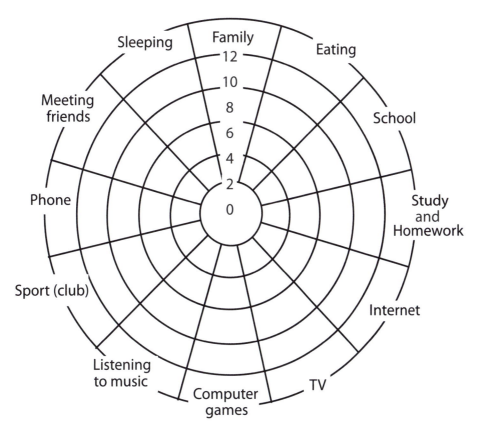

What activity do you spent most time on each day? _____

What activity do you spend the least amount of time on? _____

Which activity do you like doing best? _____

Which activity do you enjoy least? _____

Now that you are in third year, what changes could you make to your time management?

_____

_____

_____

What steps can you take to make these changes?

_____

_____

_____

Group Activity

Now that you have looked at your own time management, discuss with your group possible ways of improving how you organise your time for study. Make a list of your group's suggestions in the book below.

Organising My Timetable

A good way to help you organise your time is to draw up a work timetable.
Before you draw up your timetable, follow these steps.

1. Make a list of all your commitments, chores, favourite TV programmes,
    approximate meal times, etc.

    _____
    _____
    _____
    _____
    _____
    _____
    _____

2. Identify definite times that you can dedicate to study/project work/assignments.

    _____
    _____
    _____

3. Write a list of all your subjects.

    _____
    _____
    _____
    _____
    _____
    _____

4. Which subjects do you need to give more time to?

    _____
    _____
    _____

Guidelines for drawing up a timetable

- Be realistic: don't schedule a study slot when you know you have something else on.
- Be sure to take a break every 30–40 minutes.
- Set aside a specific time each night to study and to do your homework. This will help you establish a routine.
- Try to give more time to the subjects that you need to work harder at.
- Remember to review your timetable frequently as changes may occur in your routine.

Individual Activity

Creating My Timetable

Draw up a weekly work timetable for yourself, based on what you have written above.
Example:

Day	Subject	Time
Monday	Science English Maths	20 minutes 15 minutes 30 minutes

My Timetable

Day	Subject	Time
Monday		
Tuesday		
Wednesday		
Thursday		
Friday		
Saturday		
Sunday		

Learning *Keepsake*

Three things I have learned about organising my time are:

1. _____

2. _____

3. _____

As a result of what I have learned about organising my time I will:

_____

_____

_____

_____ has shared this Learning Keepsake with me _____

Name of student   Parent's/guardian's signature

LESSON 4
Planning for Effective Study

At the end of this lesson . . .
. . . you will have learned different ways of making studying more effective.

Key Word
- Effective
- Motivation
- Active learning

Keyskill
- Managing Myself

How to *Study*

Have you ever spent an hour studying and then wondered what you have actually learned?
Do you often find yourself reading the same page for 20 minutes?
The key to effective study is quality rather than quantity.
Read through the following text on sports nutrition as if you had to study it at home.

Sports Nutrition

Sports nutrition before, during and after training or a match.

The food that you choose to eat before, during and after training or a match can have an effect on your performance.

Before training/match

The pre-training/pre-match meal can supply your body with the energy that you need to perform at your best. You should eat the right kinds of food leading up to the event to charge your muscles with glycogen. Glycogen is a source of energy for your muscles. On the day of the game meals should mostly consist of carbohydrates (bread, potatoes, rice, pasta, cereal). Lower-fibre foods may be better tolerated on the day of the match, e.g. cornflakes, white bread, etc. Lean protein (meat, fish, eggs, nuts) should also be consumed for sustained energy. Breakfast could include wholegrain toast, cereal, porridge, boiled egg, nuts. Lunch could include rice, pasta, lean meat (e.g. chicken), fruit.

1–2 hours before training/match

You should have a light carbohydrate snack, e.g. a cereal bar, banana or small bowl of cereal. It is essential to take on water at this point and you should aim for approximately 500ml.

During exercise

It is very important to take on water every 15 to 20 minutes. Water stores are used up to cool the body through sweating. These stores need to be replenished so that the body can continue to cool down efficiently and the athlete does not lose concentration or become dehydrated.

After exercise

Your muscles are like a sponge after training and they soak up the nutrients in food. To rebuild muscles after exercise and to speed up recovery it is essential to refuel with carbohydrates or a small amount of protein within 20 minutes of finishing training or a match.

After an event it can take an athlete 20 hours or more to replace their glycogen stores. Small amounts of protein can also aid recovery. Refuelling ideas include Weetabix, cornflakes, bananas, cereal bars, smoothies, flavoured milk.

Individual Activity

1. Try to summarise what you have read on the previous page.

   _____

2. How easy or difficult did you find it to study this piece of text?

   _____
   _____
   _____

3. What techniques did you use to help you?

   _____
   _____
   _____

SQ3R

In first and second year you learned that mnemonics, mind maps and highlighting are effective techniques for active studying. The SQ3R technique is a tried and tested strategy for improving the quality of study time.

S – Survey the text by reading through it quickly to get the gist of what it says. Briefly check headings and subheadings to see what the main points are. The survey should provide you with a quick preview of everything that you need to know.

Q – Once you have read the text, ask yourself the **question**, What are the main points? This will keep you focused and help you to analyse the most important points.

R – Read through the text more slowly. Underline/highlight key words and phrases to help you recall the main points. Summarise the main points in the margins as this will make your learning active and effective. At this stage of the process mnemonics and mind maps can also aid learning.

R – Recite the main points in your own words with the book closed to check your recall. Cross-check your answers with the book. If you can't remember something, read through the text again. Make sure that you take as much time as is necessary for the information to stay in your mind.

R – Review the text every so often to fix the material in your mind. Remember to use your mnemonics and all the other techniques you know to help with your review. Looking over your work often is much more effective than one large cramming session the night before the exam. 'A little a lot is better than a lot a little.'

Individual Activity

Choose a piece of information you need to learn about and use the SQ3R technique to revise it.

Learning *Keepsake*

Three things I have learned about effective study are:

1. _____

2. _____

3. _____

As a result of what I have learned about studying effectively, I will:

_____

_____

_____

_____ has shared this Learning Keepsake with me _____

Name of student   Parent's/guardian's signature

LESSON 5
Coping with Examinations

At the end of this lesson . . .
. . . you will know your strengths and weaknesses in exams
. . . and will have developed techniques to improve your performance in exams.

Key Words
- Technique
- Examination
- Preparation

Keyskill
- Managing Myself

Before the exam

Mark is a third year student. He has just received the timetable for his Christmas exams. The exams will take place over four days. His subjects are Irish, English, Maths, Science, Music, Art, French, and CSPE. If he does not have an exam he must go to the general purpose area for study. Take a look at his timetable below and answer the questions that follow.

Year 3 Class Timetable

Monday 9 December–Thursday 12 December

Exams will take place in rooms 8, 27, 28, 41, 48, 56, 66, 68, 73, 78. Class lists and exams will be posted on classroom doors the previous day

Time	Monday	Tuesday	Wednesday	Thursday
9.00–11.00	Maths	Study English	Study Science	Study French
11.00–11.15	Break	Break	Break	Break
11.15–13.10	Study Option 1	Study CSPE	Music	Study Art
13.10–13.50	Lunch	Lunch	Lunch	Lunch
13.50–15.50	Irish	Study Option 2	Study Option 1	

Option 1	Option 2
Art – Ms Coady	Art – Mr Shortt
Business Studies – Mr Monroe	Business Studies – Ms Cusack
Home Economics – Ms Bourke	Home Economics – Mr Stuart
Materials Technology (Wood) – Mr Keyes	Materials Technology (Wood) – Ms Leahy
Technical Graphics – Ms Brazier	Music – Mr Jones

1. Write three things Mark needs to think about or do when he receives his timetable to ensure that he is well prepared for his exam.

a) _____

b) _____

c) _____

2. What subjects could Mark concentrate on at the weekend?

_____

_____

_____

3. What materials does he need to consider before doing his exams?

_____

_____

_____

On the morning of the exam

When Mark got his timetable he threw it into his bag. On Sunday night, when Mark went looking for his timetable he could not find it. He rang his friend Rory and found out that he has Maths first thing on Monday morning. Mark then remembered that he lost his calculator, but decided that he will borrow his sister's for the test. After learning his theorems Mark decided to call next door and to play on his friend's Xbox. When Mark got home he was very tired and decided to get up early the next morning to get ready for school.

On Monday Mark sleeps late. He doesn't have time to make his lunch because he has to rush out of the door to catch the bus. He asks his sister if he can borrow her calculator but she says that she has Maths at the same time. By the time Mark gets to school he realises that he hasn't checked what room the exam is in. When Mark eventually finds out where he needs to go, he is late.

During the exam

Mark is in such a hurry to start the exam that he doesn't read through all the questions and begins with the first question. Mark realises that he has chosen the wrong question as he cannot do a part of it; he should have done question 2 instead. Mark begins to get flustered and forgets stuff he definitely did know; by the time he calms down he doesn't have enough time to finish all the questions. After the exam he realises he is very hungry but hasn't brought lunch. He has only enough money to buy a small bar of chocolate and on the way to the shop he meets his friend Rory. Rory reckons he has aced the test and says that it was really easy as long as you avoided question 1.

Individual Activity

What could Mark have done before, during and after the exam to improve his performance.

Before: _____

_____

During: _____

_____

After: _____

_____

The DETER strategy for taking tests

As well as knowing the material for your exam, it is also very important to have a plan in place to help you cope with the exam. The DETER strategy can help you do your best on any test. Each letter in DETER reminds you what to do.

D = Directions

- Read the test directions very carefully and always follow the instructions on the paper. For example, if the paper says that you must 'attempt all questions', you must try to answer all the questions to stand a chance of getting full marks.
- Ask your teacher to explain anything about the test directions you do not understand.
- Only by following the directions can you achieve a good score on the test.
- If you do not follow the directions, you will not be able to demonstrate what you know.

E = Examine

- Examine the whole test; read through all the questions carefully before you begin.
- Only by knowing the entire task can you break it down into manageable parts.

T = Time

- Decide how much time you will spend on each question. Do not go over this time – once you have spent the allocated time on a question, move on, even if you have not finished. You can come back to it when you have time later on.
- Plan to spend more time on the questions with the highest marks.

E = Easiest

- The second E in DETER reminds you to answer the questions you find easiest first.
- If you get stuck on a difficult question early in the test, you might not have time to answer questions you're confident of answering well.

R = Review

- If you have planned your time correctly, you will have time to review your answers and make them as complete and accurate as possible.
- Also make sure to review the test directions to be certain you have answered all questions required.
-

Source: adapted from www.howtostudy.com

Individual Activity

1.   Create an information sheet/poster giving tips for exams

2.   Based on what you read about Mark and what you have learned about the DETER strategy, write down some changes Mark could make to help him perform better in the exam.

_____

_____

_____

_____

_____

_____

_____

_____

Learning *Keepsake*

Three things I have learned that will help me cope better with taking exams are:

1. _____
2. _____
3. _____

As a result of what I have learned about taking exams, I will:

_____
_____
_____

_____ has shared this Learning Keepsake with me _____

Name of student   Parent's/guardian's signature

LESSON 6
Making Good Decisions

At the end of this lesson . . .

. . . you will have further developed your decision-making skills

. . . and you will be aware of the importance of thinking ahead and making good decisions in relation to your education and career options.

Key Word
- Influence
- Future
- Consequences

Keyskill
- Managing Myself
- Staying Well

Decision-making

Not all decisions have serious consequences, but there are many difficult decisions in life. For example: What subjects should I choose for my Leaving Cert? Should I do Transition Year? Should I do Leaving Certificate Applied or the traditional Leaving Cert?

Because some of our decisions can affect our future, it is important to develop good decision-making skills.

In this lesson you will apply the ABCDE model of decision-making, which you learned in second year, to help Joe solve a problem he has with regard to his subject choices for the Leaving Certificate.

Meet Joe Black

Joe is in third year and he is going straight into fifth year after his Junior Certificate. Joe is very sporty, he loves science and he is an excellent guitar player. He has just received his pre-Junior Certificate results and he is very pleased with all his grades. However, Joe has a decision to make. His school is organising timetables for next year and Joe must choose his subjects. Joe is unsure about what he wants to do when he leaves school; however, he is considering a career in sport or business.

Joe Black's School Report

Christmas Exam

Class: 301

Subject	Grade	Teacher's Comment
English	B	Good work – keep it up
Irish	C	Making good progress
Maths	A	Excellent student
History	C	Will improve this grade with more work
Chinese language and Culture	D	Talkative in class
Spanish	B	Good worker
Digital Media Literacy	C	Needs to put in more effort
Business	A	Excellent student
Science	A	Excellent
Technical Graphics	D	Needs to put in more effort
Music	A	Excellent

Decisions, decisions

Joe must do English, Irish and maths; but he has to choose four more subjects so that he will have seven subjects for his Leaving Certificate.

The following factors could influence Joe's decision:

- Joe loves sports. He did some coaching over the summer and really enjoyed it.

- Joe loves history but there are two teachers, Mr Caesar and Mr Roman, for Leaving Certificate. Joe has heard that Mr Roman always gets better results. However, Joe will not find out which teacher he will get until after he chooses his subjects.
- His brother studied chemistry and told him not to choose it because it is impossible.
- He heard business is an easy subject to do well in.
- The accounting teacher is Joe's coach. Joe really likes him and heard that he is a great laugh in class.
- A couple of Joe's friends are choosing technical graphics.
- He has heard it is very hard to get an A in biology.

Now use the ABCDE model for decision-making to help point Joe in the right direction.

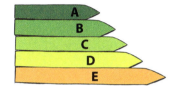

A	Assess the problem	What decision has to be made?	
B	Brainstorm the solutions	List the different options that Joe could choose.	
C	Consider the consequences of each decision	What are the consequences for Joe's future of each of the choices he could make?	
D	Decide and act	Based on the facts, the options and the consequences of each choice, suggest a list of subjects for Joe.	
E	Evaluate the consequences	Explain the pros and cons of the suggested list.	

After going through the ABCDE process, what subjects would you advise Joe to take?
1. English
2. Irish
3. Maths
4. _____
5. _____
6. _____
7. _____

Class Activity

1. How difficult was it to choose Joe's subjects?
2. What other decisions do people have to make about their study and future careers?
3. What important decisions have you made about your education?

Individual Activity

Now that you have helped Joe to decide on his subjects, identify an important decision that you must make about your own future education. Follow the ABCDE decision-making process to help you make up your mind.

A	Assess the problem	What decision has to be made?	
B	Brainstorm the solutions	List the different options that you can choose from.	
C	Consider the consequences of each decision	What are the consequences for your future of each of the choices you could make?	
D	Decide and act	Based on the facts and the options open to you, make a decision about what you will do.	
E	Evaluate the consequences	Explain the pros and cons of your final choice(s).	

Learning *Keepsake*

Three things I have learned about making good decisions are:

1. _____
2. _____
3. _____

As a result of what I have learned about making decisions, I will:

_____

_____

_____

_____ has shared this Learning Keepsake with me _____

Name of student   Parent's/guardian's signature

Topic Review

Date / /

In this topic I learned about

_____

This topic is useful to me in my life because

_____

_____

In this topic I liked

_____

_____

In this topic I did not like

_____

_____

I would like to find out more about

_____

_____

Key Skills I have used in this topic are:

☐ Managing myself
☐ Staying well
☐ Communicating
☐ Being creative
☐ Working with others
☐ Managing information and thinking

*Are you up for the challenge?

Design a page for your school journal/website giving tips for effective study.

TOPIC 3

Respectful Communication

LESSON 7
Learning to Communicate

At the end of this lesson . . .
. . . you will have further developed your communication skills in sensitive situations.

Key Words
- Sensitive
- Communication

Keyskill
- Communicating

Sometimes we face situations in which we find it difficult to talk or don't know what to say. This does not mean that we should ignore the situation or avoid talking about it.

At difficult times someone may not want to talk, and you must be sensitive to this. If the person is someone you know really well and you have a very good relationship you can only really know how they are feeling by asking them. It is important that you choose the right time. Remember, people don't always want to be told what to do, but you can help them explore their options. You could be a good source of support for someone.

Individual Activity

Give three examples of sensitive situations a person your age might have to deal with. Example: Talking to someone after the death of a loved one.

1. _____

2. _____

3. _____

Group Activity

Read the story your teacher assigns to your group and answer the questions below.

1. Over the holidays your friend's grandfather died. Your friend lived with his grandfather, and they were very close. You haven't seen him over the holidays. Now that you are back at school you feel uncomfortable around him because you didn't go to the funeral.

2. Your friend is going out with a boy from your class. She calls to your house and is very upset because her boyfriend has broken up with her. You feel relieved because you heard rumours that he has been cheating on her with someone in fifth year.

3. You and your best friend have known each other since crèche. You are great friends. People often laugh and say that you are 'joined at the hip'. You share everything – secrets, stories, video games. For the last few weeks, however, you've noticed that your friend doesn't seem happy: they have started to do badly in school tests; and sometimes they fly off the handle for the slightest thing. You found out last night that your friend's parents have separated. You can't believe your friend didn't tell you.

4. Your friend has been fainting a lot at school. You notice that she has lost weight. She often says to other people that she's fat. You have started paying attention to what she is eating. Yesterday she only ate an apple and a yoghurt for lunch. You are concerned for her, but you are not sure how she will react if you say something.

5. It is a week to go before the end of the Easter holidays. You get a text from a school friend. In the text your friend tells you that he is gay. He tells you that he has come out to his family and friends, but you are the first person he has told from school. He tells you it won't be long before other people at school find out, and he is nervous because he doesn't know how people will react.

6. Your best friend's grandmother has just died. She was very close to her grandmother, who was very old and living in a nursing home, and she is very upset. She told you when the funeral was, but you didn't even know her grandmother. The fact is, you don't know what to say to her or even how to behave at a funeral.

How do you think your friend is feeling?
_____
_____

What could you say in this situation?
_____
_____

When would be a good time to say something?
_____
_____

How comfortable would you feel discussing this?
_____
_____

Why might you choose not to say anything?
_____
_____

How good do you think you are at dealing with sensitive situations?
_____
_____

Class Activity

When you have finished answering the questions, discuss them with your class.

Tips for dealing with sensitive situations

- **Don't be afraid to ask:** They will tell you if they are not ready to talk.

- **Choose the right time:** It is very important to choose the right time and place to talk to someone. For example, bringing up a sensitive issue such as grief when the person seems to be having fun is not a good idea.

- **Be sympathetic:** Let the person know that you realise it is a difficult situation for them, e.g. say things like 'It must be difficult for you,' or 'Is there anything I can do?' Don't tell them how they should be feeling.

- **Listen – try not to talk too much:** Give the person time to say how they are feeling.

- **Spot the clues:** Have they said something in passing that they hope you will ask them about? If someone brings up a sensitive situation, don't just change the subject.

- **Choose the right questions:** Choose questions that will encourage them to talk. Ask questions starting with 'How . . .', 'What . . .', 'Where . . .', 'When . . .' and 'Why . . .', e.g. 'How do you feel about . . .?', 'What was it like for you?'

- **Avoid closed questions:** These are questions that only need one-word answers. They are also known as conversation stoppers. Examples: 'Are you upset?' 'Yes.' 'Do you think you'll tell her?'

- **Use body language:** Be relaxed, make eye contact, have appropriate facial expressions.

- **If the other person gets upset:** Don't overreact; stay calm. Don't feel you have the answers – they may just want you to listen.

Role Play

In pairs, choose one of the scenarios from pages 39-40. Write a role play for it using the tips for sensitive communication.

While one pair is doing their role play, the rest of the class will fill in the observation sheet below.

Observation sheet

How sensitive was the person in dealing with the situation? What makes you say this?

_____

_____

Do you think they were helpful in the advice they gave? Give reasons.

_____

_____

Is there anything that could have been done differently?

_____

_____

Learning *Keepsake*

Three things I have learned about sensitive communication are:

1. _____

2. _____

3. _____

As a result of what I have learned about sensitive communication, I will:

_____

_____

_____

_____ has shared this Learning Keepsake with me _____

Name of student   Parent's/guardian's signature

LESSON 8
Constructive Criticism

At the end of this lesson . . .
. . . you will have evaluated the role of constructive criticism in your life
. . . and enhanced your skills in dealing with conflict.

Key Words
- Feedback
- Constructive criticism
- Destructive criticism

Keyskill
- Communicating

Giving and receiving constructive feedback

Throughout our lives we receive feedback in many different ways – we get both compliments and criticism.

Constructive criticism is criticism which is well meant and has the goal of improving some area of another person's life or work. A coach might say, 'You're not match fit – you have good skills, but you need to work on your fitness to make the team.'

Destructive criticism has the sole purpose of insulting or hurting the other person, e.g. 'You played so badly in the basketball game today.'

Look at the following statements and tick whether you think they are an example of constructive or destructive criticism:

	Constructive	Destructive
Oh my God, the state of your hair! (stranger at school)	☐	☐
Wake up! You're not tuned in! (teacher)	☐	☐
I have never seen you looking so tired. (boyfriend/girlfriend)	☐	☐
If you only worked harder you'd get on the team. (coach)	☐	☐
You don't know your lines, so you can't act in the play. (friend)	☐	☐
You are so rude to your parents! (boy/girlfriend)	☐	☐
You need to go away and eat something, you skinny cow. (brother)	☐	☐
You haven't got a note in your head! (mother)	☐	☐
Oh my God, what are you wearing? (friend)	☐	☐
You drive too fast! (friend)	☐	☐

 Class Activity

1. Which of these statements are most likely to be hurtful?
2. Which of these statements could help a person to improve?
3. How easy is it to identify which of these statements are helpful?
4. How does a person's tone of voice and body language affect the message they are trying to communicate?

The way you communicate constructive criticism will determine how well the other person takes it.

Write an example of when someone your age might give constructive criticism to someone and an example of when someone your age might receive constructive criticism.

The Sandwich Rule for giving constructive feedback

1. When giving constructive criticism we can compare it to making a sandwich. Firstly we give a compliment, this is the top slice of the sandwich.

2. Secondly, add the criticism which represents the meat filling of the sandwich.

3. Finally add the second compliment which is the final slice in the sandwich.

Some guidelines for giving constructive criticism

In addition to the Sandwich Rule, the following guidelines are important for delivering constructive criticism.

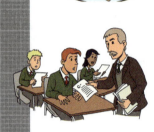

- Choose the right time and place.
- Be sensitive to the other person.
- Make sure that there aren't a lot of other people present.
- Don't raise your voice; speak calmly.
- The tone of your voice should indicate that you are trying to help.
- Use 'I' statements ('I feel . . .', 'I think . . .', etc.), not 'You' statements ('You never . . .', 'You should . . .', etc.).

The following tips are helpful for dealing with constructive criticism.

- Stay calm.
- Listen to the other person's point of view.
- Think before responding.
- Consider why the person is giving the criticism.
- Don't become defensive.
- Ask yourself: what can I learn from the criticism?
- Respond to the criticism using 'I' statements.

 Group Activity

Using the Sandwich Rule for delivering constructive feedback, identify reasons why the feedback in each case below is not effectively delivered.

Suggest how you could give the criticism in a constructive manner in each case.

Learning *Keepsake*

Three things I have learned about constructive criticism are:

1. _____
2. _____
3. _____

As a result of what I have learned about constructive criticism, I will:

_____
_____
_____

_____ has shared this Learning Keepsake with me _____

Name of student   Parent's/guardian's signature

LESSON 9
Your Style in Conflict

At the end of this lesson . . .

. . . you will have identified sources of conflict in your life

. . . you will recognise how you behave in conflict situations

. . . you will be able to evaluate the strengths and weaknesses of how you deal with conflict

. . . you will and have improved your skills in dealing with conflict.

Key Words
- Conflict
- Resolution

Keyskill
- Communication

Your parents demand that you clean your room. Someone skips ahead of you in a queue. Your closest friend starts seeing a guy she knows you like. Your teacher unfairly accuses you. A player from the other team insults you off the ball during a soccer game. All of these scenarios can lead to conflict.

Group Activity

Give other examples of when conflict might arise for someone your age in everyday life.

People respond to conflict in different ways, depending on the situation. For example, you might react one way with you parents and another with your friends. What you are like in public might be very different from what you are like in private. Most of us have our own way of reacting to conflict.

What is your style in conflict?

Each statement below corresponds to a particular way that people deal with conflict. Beside each statement give a rating between 1 and 4:

- 1 = very unlike me
- 2 = unlike me
- 3 = like me
- 4 = very like me

Statement	Score
1. I listen to others and I make sure that everyone is heard.	
2. I usually do what other people expect me to.	
3. I usually argue my point until I get what I want.	
4. I walk away from the situation to avoid tension.	
5. I usually meet people half way.	
6. I prefer not to hurt people's feelings.	
7. I prefer to stay out of conflict.	
8. I don't back down in arguments.	
9. I usually allow other people to get their way and I back down.	
10. I am always happy to give up something to resolve the problem.	
11. I love a good argument.	
12. I like to listen to everyone's side and then try to solve the problem.	
13. I usually sit down and discuss the issue openly.	
14. If people don't respect my opinion I keep it to myself.	
15. In most situations I think something is better than nothing.	

Scoring instructions:

The 15 statements on the previous correspond to the five different ways of dealing with conflict. To find your preferred style, total the points you scored in each category. The one with the highest score is your preferred style.

Style		Add your scores for questions:	Your total score
Turtle	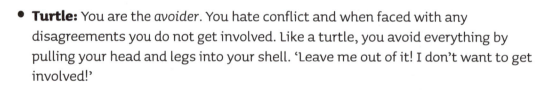	4, 7, 14	
Lion		3, 8, 11	
Zebra		5, 10, 15	
Chameleon		2, 6, 9	
Dolphin		1, 12, 13	

Which style/styles are you?

_____

- **Turtle:** You are the *avoider*. You hate conflict and when faced with any disagreements you do not get involved. Like a turtle, you avoid everything by pulling your head and legs into your shell. 'Leave me out of it! I don't want to get involved!'

- **Lion:** The king of the jungle. You are the *attacker*. You are right and everyone else is wrong. You don't listen to or accept anyone else's point of view. Like the lion, you use your roar and your strength to get your way. 'I'm telling you! I know I'm right!'

- **Zebra:** You are the *compromiser*. You always give up something to help reach an agreement. Whether right or wrong, you always compromise – an admirable strategy; you meet people half way. Like the zebra, you don't care if you're a black horse or a white horse. 'Let's split the difference. If you agree to this, I'll agree to that.'

- **Chameleon:** The *people pleaser*. Giving in and agreeing with the other is your preferred style. It's better to be liked than to be truly honest. You believe that keeping a good friend is more important than anything else. Like the chameleon, you change your colour to suit your environment. 'Your friendship means more to me than this. I'll get over it.'

- **Dolphin:** Mr/Ms *Co-operative*! You value everyone's opinion. You listen to the other person's point of view. You are willing to listen and work together for a solution that's best for everyone involved. Like dolphins, you work together. 'I'm sure if we work together we can figure this out.'

The way we deal with conflict varies from situation to situation, and from person to person. The style we use is not fixed – it can change from one situation to the next. You may be a lion in one circumstance and a turtle in another. Although we've used the animal analogy, you are not an animal and you have the power to change. Effective conflict resolution requires us to consider each person's viewpoint and feelings. Write down the advantages and disadvantages of your style of conflict resolution.

Style _____

Advantages	Disadvantages

Me in Conflict

Think of a time when you were in a conflict situation. What was it about?

_____

_____

What style did you adopt?

_____

_____

If you were in the same situation again, would you do the same thing? Why/why not?

_____

_____

_____

_____

Learning *Keepsake*

Three things I have learned about conflict are:

1. _____
2. _____
3. _____

As a result of what I have learned about conflict, I will:

_____
_____
_____

_____ has shared this Learning Keepsake with me _____
Name of student   Parent's/guardian's signature

LESSON 10
Dealing with Conflict

At the end of this lesson . . .
. . . you will have further developed your conflict resolution skills.

Key Words
- Conflict
- Resolution

 # Keyskill
- Communicating

Conflict Resolution

Conflict is a normal part of everyday life. The important question, then, is not so much how we avoid conflict, but rather how we manage it as positively as possible.

 Pair Activity

Your teacher will assign you pictures from the below. Answer the questions that follow.

What do you think the conflict is about?

_____

_____

Describe how each person could be feeling.

_____

_____

_____

_____

What could happen for each scenario to end in an argument?

_____

_____

What needs to happen so that the situation is resolved and all parties are happy?

_____

_____

How to deal with conflict situations: some advice

Four steps for dealing with conflict are to keep calm, deal with the issue, listen and work it out.

Step 1 Keep calm
- Count to 10.
- Take deep breaths.

Step 2 Deal with the issue
- Choose a suitable time and place to talk.
- Don't raise your voice. Speak calmly.
- Use 'I' statements.
- Keep the conflict between you and the other person or people who are directly involved. Don't ask friends to take sides.

'I' and 'You'
One of the most effective ways of resolving conflict is to use 'I' statements. Often when people engage in conflict they attack and blame the other person, e.g. 'You never want to hang out with me any more.' This can often lead to the accused person responding in a defensive or aggressive manner. 'I' statements help to tackle conflict in an unthreatening, tactful way.

Convert the following 'You' statements to 'I' statements.

'You . . .'	'I . . .'
1. You always pick on me.	I feel singled out when you call on me more than other students.
2. You never help me tidy up.	
3. You never spend time with me.	
4. You always take my things without asking.	
5. You always put me down.	
6. You're always asking me to cover for you.	
7. You're never happy with anything I do.	
8. You're so selfish.	
9. You're rude and inconsiderate.	
10. You make me so angry.	

Step 3 Listen
- Listen to each other, take turns and consider the other person's side of the story.
- Don't interrupt or be defensive.
- Try to see where the other person is coming from. Put yourself in their shoes.

Step 4 Work it out
- Talk things through and come to an agreement that both of you are happy with.
- Sometimes you may be unable to reach a satisfactory resolution and it may be necessary to walk away and seek help from a parent, teacher, etc.

 Role Play

Your teacher will assign you one of the scenarios on the next page. Using your scenario role play a conversation in which the two individuals resolve the conflict. Use all you have learned about conflict management.

1. Friend troubles

My friend Valerie is normally kind and supportive. Recently we have started hanging out with a new group of friends. When she is in their company her mood seems different. Every time I say something she embarrasses me, puts me down or disagrees with me. She has always been a good friend to me. I don't understand her behaviour and it's very hurtful.

2. Show me the money

I lent my friend George €30 from my birthday money five weeks ago. I haven't asked him for the money back. I know he started a part-time job two weeks ago and I feel that he now has the cash to pay me back. What should I say?

3. Caught out

My friend Jennifer is always asking me to cover for her when she goes out. Several times she has told her parents that she is staying at my house when in fact she's out drinking with other friends. I met her mother in the shop last week and it was really awkward. What should I say to her?

4. Music to my ears

Patrick bought a new iPod, which his younger brother Joe is always asking to borrow. One day his brother borrowed the iPod without permission, accidentally dropped it and cracked the screen. He secretly returned it, in the hope that his brother wouldn't know it was him. When Patrick discovered the iPod he was furious: he had saved up for months to buy the iPod and he couldn't believe his brother had been so careless. He storms into Joe's room and shoves him against the wall.

5. Gossip girl

Sarah and Emma have been friends for the past two years. Recently, however, Sarah has heard that Emma has been talking about her behind her back. Sarah is really upset and decides to talk to Emma about this.

6. Teacher trouble

John is a hard-working student and always does his best. But John feels that in the past few weeks his English teacher has been treating him unfairly during class, and he thinks that his teacher is being overly critical of his work. He would even go so far as to say that the teacher has been making fun of him.

Role play reflection:

1. Which scenario were you assigned? _____

2. What was the most difficult aspect of the role play?

   _____

   _____

Learning *Keepsake*

Three things I have learned about conflict resolution are:

1. _____
2. _____
3. _____

As a result of what I have learned about resolving conflicts, I will:

_____
_____
_____

_____ has shared this Learning Keepsake with me _____
Name of student   Parent's/guardian's signature

Topic Review

Date / /

In this topic I learned about
_____
_____

This topic is useful to me in my life because
_____
_____
_____

In this topic I liked
_____
_____
_____

In this topic I did not like
_____
_____
_____

I would like to find out more about
_____
_____
_____

Key Skills I have used in this topic are:

☐ Managing myself
☐ Staying well
☐ Communicating
☐ Being creative
☐ Working with others
☐ Managing information and thinking

*Are you up for the challenge?

Identify in groups a conflict situation you have seen involving a young person and critique it. Write out and role play a scene which demonstrates conflict resolution.

TOPIC 4

Being Healthy

LESSON 11
Healthy Eating

At the end of this lesson . . .
. . . you will have reflected on your diet
. . . you will know the difference between a healthy and an unhealthy diet
. . . and you will understand the consequences of a poor diet.

Key Words
- Advertising
- Crash diets

Keyskill
- Staying Well

Advertisements *and Food*

Class Activity

1. What are these advertisements selling?
2. What techniques are they using to persuade you to buy their product?
3. Can you think of other advertisements that persuade young people to buy certain foods? What persuasive methods do the advertisers use?

Why we eat

There are many different reasons why we eat. We often eat for reasons other than nutrition and refuelling, for example at social occasions or out of boredom or stress. When you were younger, your parents influenced what you ate. During adolescence you have more pocket money and therefore more opportunities to choose your own foods. It is very important to make healthy food choices. Sometimes, however, young people can slip into bad eating habits. These can include:

- skipping breakfast
- snacking on junk food
- eating fast food

- crash dieting/skipping meals
- eating large portion sizes
- drinking sugary drinks

Write down the factors you think influence these poor eating habits.

Poor eating habit	Influencing factors
Skipping breakfast	
Snacking on junk food	
Eating fast food	
Crash dieting/skipping meals	
Eating large portions	
Drinking sugary drinks	

Healthy eating guidelines

Look at the following guidelines for healthy eating.

Start the day the right way

A good breakfast sets you up for the rest of the day and kick-starts your metabolism, i.e. your body's ability to burn fat/calories. People who eat breakfast have a healthier body weight than those who skip it. Eating a healthy breakfast helps you to concentrate better at school.

Eat fresh rather than processed food

Instead of snacking on chocolate, crisps and sugary foods, choose fruit and healthy snacks. Here are some examples of healthy snacks you could choose from:

- fresh fruit or vegetable sticks
- popcorn
- fruit or wholemeal scone
- nuts
- wholegrain cereal bar
- yoghurts
- wholegrain crackers.

Avoid eating fast food

Fast food is processed and contains a lot of fat, sugar and salt. The recommended salt intake for teenagers is less than 1 teaspoon per day. Remember that processed foods often contain hidden salt. Eighty-six per cent of men and 67% of women eat too much salt. Excess salt is linked with high blood pressure, which can lead to heart disease, stroke and obesity.

Avoid crash dieting

Ninety-five per cent of diets do not work and people regain the weight they lose. However, crash dieting to lose weight can be common among young people, particularly girls.

When you go on a crash diet your body begins to believe it is starving, so it goes into survival mode. When you eat something it stores it as fat, in case you starve it again.

Know your portion size

Cutting down on portion sizes is a good start to eating healthily. Try to avoid large packets of crisps or king-size bars. You don't have to keep eating until you burst; try to recognise when you have satisfied your hunger. It takes the brain twenty minutes to register that we are full, so eat slowly and chew your food.

Cut down on sugary drinks/drink more milk and water

Sports drinks and fizzy drinks contain a lot of sugar – for example, one 330ml bottle of Lucozade contains 12.5 teaspoons of sugar and a can of normal Coke contains 11 teaspoons of sugar. Water and milk are the most suitable drinks for someone your age. It is recommended that we drink eight glasses of water every day.

Small changes can make a big difference

Look at some small changes you could make to your mealtimes.

Swap this	Swap this	Swap this	Swap this	Swap this
Sugar-coated cereals	Ready meals/fast foods	White bread meat sandwich and large chocolate bar	Battered fish, chips and portion of beans	Crisps (45g bag)

For this	**For this**	**For this**	**For this**	**For this**
Bowl of corn flakes and a glass of orange juice	Medium white roll with breaded chicken	Brown bread meat sandwich, piece of fruit and snack size chocolate bar	Fish fillet, beans, and chips	Crisps (25g bag)

Better still this	**Better still this**	**Better still this**	**Better still this**	**Better still this**
Small bowl of porridge with fresh fruit and a glass of orange juice	Medium white roll with plain chicken fillet and salad	Brown bread meat and salad sandwich, piece of fruit and low fat yoghurt.	Swap chips for wedges and add more veg	Small bowl of pop corn

Source: www.littlesteps.eu

Now think about any unhealthy food choices you make and decide how to swap these unhealthy choices for healthier ones. Remember, making small changes can make a big difference.

Unhealthy choices I make	. . . swap for . . .	Healthier choice
Breakfast	→	
Break time	→	
Lunch	→	
Dinner	→	
Snacks	→	

Learning *Keepsake*

Three things I have learned about a healthy diet are:

1. _____
2. _____
3. _____

As a result of what I have learned about a healthy diet, I will:

_____
_____
_____

_____ has shared this Learning Keepsake with me _____
Name of student   Parent's/guardian's signature

LESSON 12
Physical Exercise

At the end of this lesson . . .
. . . you will appreciate the need for physical exercise in your life

. . . you will have reflected on your current activity levels

. . . and you will have planned an exercise programme that suits your life.

Key Words
- Physically active
- Recreational activities
- Moderate exercise
- Vigorous exercise

Keyskill
- Staying Well

How active are you?

Complete the quiz to determine how active you are. For each question, circle the answer that best applies to you.

1. How many days per week would you do 60 minutes of moderate to vigorous activity?
   a) 5 or more
   b) 2-4
   c) 0–1

2. How would you describe your fitness level?
   a) Very fit
   b) Quite fit
   c) Very unfit

3. When you are out and about, do you normally:
   a) Take the stairs?
   b) Take the lift and walk?
   c) Take the lift?

4. Are you physically active at home, e.g. would you walk to the shop, walk the dog, do the Hoovering, mow the lawn:
   a) Most of the time
   b) Sometimes, but only when I have to
   c) Never

5. During break at school, do you spend most of your time:
   a) Doing an activity in the playground?
   b) Walking around the corridors with friends?
   c) Sitting down talking to friends?

6. How would you describe your participation in PE class?
   a) I love PE and I rarely miss it
   b) I like doing it most of the time depending on the activity
   c) I usually try to get out of it by forgetting my gear or bringing in a note

7. How would you describe your attitude to physical activity?
   a) I enjoy being physically active; it is a big part of my life
   b) I don't mind exercise but I find it difficult to fit it into my day
   c) I don't like sports or physical activity; I prefer to spend my spare time watching TV, listening to music or playing computer games

8. When you exercise, how do you feel?

a) My heart rate is very fast and I'm sweating and breathing heavily

b) My heart rate is faster and I'm slightly out of breath but I can still carry on a conversation

c) More or less the same as I do when I'm not exercising

9. How many times per week do you do flexibility, muscle-strengthening and bone-strengthening exercises (e.g. stretches, sit ups, bicep curls, skipping)?

a) 2–3

b) 0–1

c) Never

10. Do you take part in physical activities in your leisure time (e.g. walking, cycling, dancing, sports)?

a) Most days

b) Sometimes

c) Never

Your score:

If you circled mostly a's: Well done! Keep up this level of activity in your daily routine.
If you circled mostly b's: You have made a good start. Now try to increase the amount of activity you do each week.
If you circled mostly c's: You need to get more active.

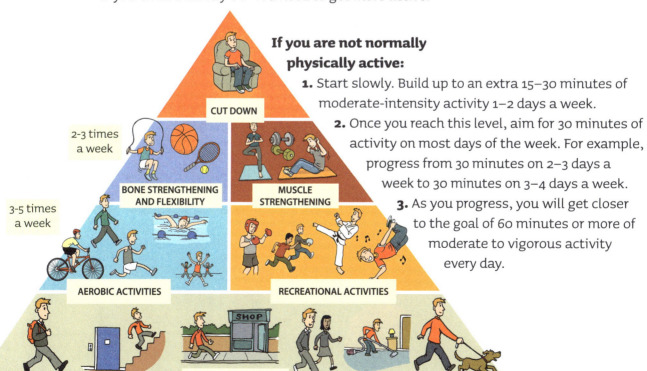

If you are not normally physically active:

1. Start slowly. Build up to an extra 15–30 minutes of moderate-intensity activity 1–2 days a week.

2. Once you reach this level, aim for 30 minutes of activity on most days of the week. For example, progress from 30 minutes on 2–3 days a week to 30 minutes on 3–4 days a week.

3. As you progress, you will get closer to the goal of 60 minutes or more of moderate to vigorous activity every day.

2-3 times a week

3-5 times a week

CUT DOWN

BONE STRENGTHENING AND FLEXIBILITY

MUSCLE STRENGTHENING

AEROBIC ACTIVITIES

RECREATIONAL ACTIVITIES

EVERYDAY ACTIVITIES

Source: *Get Ireland Active: Promoting Physical Activity in Ireland*, HSE.

Activity plan

Using the activity pyramid as a guide, draw up a plan for one week that matches your present level of activity.

Ask yourself:
- Why am I exercising? (To keep fit or to train for a specific sport, for example.)
- What time of the day does it suit me best to exercise?
- What types of activity do I like?
- Do I prefer to exercise with friends or alone?
- How will I overcome any obstacles to my exercising?

Activity Timetable

Day	Goal	Type of exercise	Duration of exercise	How I did
Monday				
Tuesday				
Wednesday				
Thursday				
Friday				
Saturday				
Sunday				

Learning *Keepsake*

Three things I have learned about being active are:

1. _____
2. _____
3. _____

As a result of what I have learned about being active, I will:

_____
_____
_____

_____ has shared this Learning Keepsake with me _____

Name of student   Parent's/guardian's signature

LESSON 13
Relaxation

At the end of this lesson . . .
. . . you will appreciate the importance of relaxation
. . . and you will have learned and practised some
relaxation techniques.

Key Words
- Guided relaxation

Keyskill
- Staying Well

In order to be healthy it is important to balance physical and mental activity with rest and relaxation. If we are very busy, we can experience stress. It is important to have some stress-releasing activities to help to stay calm during stressful times.

What type of activities do you like to do to help you relax? Listening to music, counting to ten, taking deep slow breaths? Think of the things you do now when you need to stay calm or relax and write them into the clouds.

Learning to relax

Most young people lead very busy lives following timetables, getting work done and developing their skills and hobbies. Even when things are going well, teenagers need to build relaxation into their routine. Taking time out to relax can prevent you becoming overwhelmed in stressful situations. When people become overwhelmed they can often forget to breathe: deep breathing can really help a person cope with a stressful situation.

Deep breathing exercise

Get comfortable, sitting upright on a chair or lying on the floor on a mat. Place your hand on your abdomen. Take a slow deep breath in through your nose, noticing your hand moving outwards. Hold your breath for a count of three, then breathe out. Concentrate on your breathing. Notice that as you breathe out the tension is released. The calmest or quietest time in this process is immediately after you breathe out. Take note of the calmness in your body at this point.

What was it like for you to concentrate on your breathing?

_____

_____

Did you find it easy or difficult to do this breathing exercise?

_____

_____

Can you think of situations in which deep breathing could be helpful?

_____

_____

Relaxation techniques

Here are some different types of popular relaxation techniques. You should aim to do a relaxation exercise for about ten minutes every day. These can be built into your day.

1. Breathing exercise

- Breathe in. Hold for a count of three.
- When you breathe out again, say 'ten,' letting go of tension as if it is being carried out of your body with the air.
- Next time you breathe out, say 'nine,' and so on, all the way down to 'one.'
- When you get to 'one,' start again.
- Each time you breathe out, tell yourself you are letting go of tension.
- Many people repeat this sequence slowly for a period of 15 to 20 minutes. They find that with each new countdown, they reach a deeper level of relaxation.

2. Mindfulness

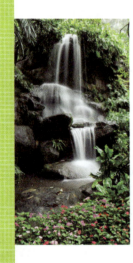

- Sit comfortably.
- Listen to your breathing.
- Pay all your attention to your breath.
- Let any thoughts you have pass through. Acknowledge them but don't judge them.
- Keep your concentration on your breathing.

3. Guided Imagery: Imagining a calm place

This is another very effective way of helping us to relax. With this method you imagine yourself in a place where you feel happy or peaceful. You can do this activity on your own or using CDs.

- Find a comfortable place free from distraction.
- Close your eyes.
- If you wish, you can play some soothing gentle music. It is probably better if you choose music with no lyrics.
- Imagine a place where you feel completely happy and relaxed – your happy place. Choose a place you find calming: perhaps your garden, your bedroom, a place where you had a great holiday, a favourite childhood spot. It could also be an imaginary setting, e.g. a tropical beach.
- Look around you – take in what you are seeing, the colours and the shapes.
- Pay attention to the sounds you hear: listen carefully to the wind blowing, waves crashing, seagulls calling, etc.
- Reach out and touch things around you.
- Be aware of any smells.
- Now stay in this place for a while. Notice how relaxed you feel, how free of tension your body feels.
- Repeat in your head, 'I am relaxed, I am happy', 'I am a great person', 'Life is good.'

4. Progressive muscule relaxation

Get comfortable. Lie on the floor or on a firm bed, or sit in a chair that has good head support.

- Close your eyes and breathe deeply two or three times.
- Start with your face. Squint your eyes, tighten your jaws and wrinkle your forehead. Feel the tension while you count silently to five, and then let go of it. Feel the warmth of relaxation coming to your face.
- Next, pull your shoulders up until they nearly touch your ears. Feel the tension while you count silently to five. Then let go.
- Now continue down the rest of your body, tightening muscles as you go and counting slowly to five each time. Start with your hands, followed by your stomach, then work down to your thighs, and finish with your lower legs, curling up your toes and tightening calf muscles to feel the tension in your feet, ankles, calves and knees.

When you have finished, notice the sense of release in all your muscles. Breathe deeply a few times, and feel relaxed, refreshed and comfortable.

Teacher's Book

Sit comfortably in your chair. Your teacher will now bring you through a relaxation technique.

Now that you have participated in a relaxation exercise, answer the following questions.

1. How did you feel before you listened to the audio?

   _____
   _____

2. How did you feel after you listened to the audio?

   _____
   _____

3. What was your favourite part of the relaxation technique?

   _____
   _____

4. What background sounds did you hear?

   _____
   _____

5. What do you think are the benefits, if any, of listening to the relaxation audio?

   _____
   _____

Learning *Keepsake*

Three things I have learned about relaxation are:

1. _____
2. _____
3. _____

As a result of what I have learned about relaxation, I will:

_____
_____
_____

_____ has shared this Learning Keepsake with me _____

Name of student   Parent's/guardian's signature

LESSON 14
Recognising Unsafe Situations

Key Words
- Risk
- Safety

Keyskill
- Staying Safe

Personal safety

Now that you are older you have more independence and more responsibility for your own personal safety. It is important to recognise possible unsafe situations when you encounter them. You should avoid getting yourself into situations that you may not be able to deal with.

Here are four situations that any teenager might normally find themselves in. Write down possible dangers that could arise in each situation.

A Suzy is babysitting for the Smiths, who live one mile away from her house. The Smiths have told Suzy that they will be home quite late. The telephone rings and it is a man looking for Mr Smith.

B Joe's parents have decided to go out for the evening. This means that Joe is alone in the house. Joe goes on to Facebook and puts out an open invitation to a house party.

C Martin does after-school study and doesn't leave the school building until 6.30 p.m. One evening on his way home some of the lads drive by in John's father's car. John is driving and pulls down the window to offer Martin a lift.

D Lucy has just returned from visiting her aunt. Lucy's mother was due to collect her at half past nine. However, the train has pulled into the station a little early. The battery on Lucy's phone has died and she has no way of contacting her mother. The train station is very empty and quiet.

A _____
_____
_____
_____

B _____
_____
_____
_____

C _____
_____
_____
_____

D _____
_____
_____
_____

Individual Activity

1. Were you ever in an everyday situation (e.g. on public transport, walking down the street, playing a match, etc.) that posed some threat to your personal safety?

_____

_____

_____

2. Choose one of the scenarios A, B, C or D above and outline what advice you would give to maximise the personal safety of the person involved.

_____

_____

_____

Some tips

Here are some tips for helping to safeguard a young person's personal safety:

- When babysitting, never admit to being on your own in a house.
- Do not answer any unexpected calls to the door, unless you are sure it's someone you trust.
- Never put personal information on a social networking site. This includes saying that you have a free house.
- Only ever accept a lift from a responsible driver. If you have any doubts, be assertive and just say no.
- Do not carry all your belongings in one bag. Make sure your personal possessions – e.g. keys, phone, wallet – are kept securely.
- If you are using public transport, always sit near the driver and avoid waiting or travelling in isolated places.
- If you are worried about your personal safety, go to the nearest place where there are people and call the Gardaí.

Now add any other safety tips you can think of from your own experience.

Personal safety quiz

Answer the following questions by putting a circle around the correct answer.

1. **You have been out with your friends. It is late and you are on your way home alone. You should:**
    A. Take any shortcuts to get you home quicker.
    B. Take the quietest route because it is safer when there is no one around to cause trouble.
    C. Take the busiest route home because there is safety in numbers.

2. **It is always important to plan how you will get to and from your destination because:**
   A. You can plan to have safe places along the route.
   B. You won't get lost.
   C. Both of the above.

3. **If your instincts tell you that you are in danger you should:**
   A. Get out of the situation without delay.
   B. Wait a little while in case you are imagining it.
   C. Ignore the feeling: it would be too embarrassing if you were wrong.

4. **When waiting for public transport or a lift you should:**
   A. Wait near other people in a well-lit area.
   B. Wait in a quiet area where no one will see you.
   C. Find a person you like the look of and stand near them.

5. **When travelling in a car or on a train you should:**
   A. Never sit near the driver.
   B. Sit away from other people to avoid any trouble.
   C. Sit as close to the driver as possible.

6. **You are on a train and someone sits next to you. They make you feel distinctly uncomfortable. You should:**
   A. Avoid eye contact and pointedly ignore the person.
   B. Move to another seat or carriage.
   C. Text your friend that you are sitting next to a weirdo.

7. **You receive a threatening message on your phone. You should:**
   A. Tell an adult whom you trust.
   B. Ignore and delete the message.
   C. Send a threat back to the other person.

8. **You are having a small get-together with your friends. How should you invite the people you would like to be there?**
   A. Send them a text message.
   B. Put it up on Facebook so that everyone will see it.
   C. Meet your friends personally and invite them.

Now add up your scores:

Q1. a = 0 b = 0 c = 3
Q2. a = 1 b =1 c = 3
Q3. a =3 b = 0 c = 0
Q4. a = 3 b = 0 c = 0
Q5. a = 0 b = 0 c = 3
Q6. a = 0 b = 3 c = 0
Q7. a = 3 b =0 c = 0
Q8. a = 3 b = 0 c = 0

- If you scored between 0 and 14, you need to improve the steps you take to increase your personal safety.
- If you scored between 15 and 20, you are quite safety-conscious, but there is room for improvement.
- If you scored between 20 and 24, you are safety aware. Well done!

Learning *Keepsake*

Three things I have learned about personal safety are:

1. _____
2. _____
3. _____

As a result of what I have learned about personal safety, I will:

_____
_____
_____

_____ has shared this Learning Keepsake with me _____
Name of student   Parent's/guardian's signature

LESSON 15
Violence

At the end of this lesson . . .

. . . you will be conscious of violence as a threat to personal and group safety

. . . you will have examined ways of avoiding potentially violent situations

. . . and you will have developed some skills for handling violent situations.

Key Word
- Violence

 # Keyskill
- Staying Safe

Violence

Violence can be **psychological** or **physical**.

- **Psychological violence** includes emotional blackmail, bullying, intimidation and verbal abuse.
- **Physical violence** includes physical attack and sexual assault.

The World Health Organisation (WHO) defines violence as the 'intentional use of physical force or power, threatened or actual, against oneself, against another person, or against a group or community, which either results in or has a high likelihood of resulting in injury, death, psychological harm, maldevelopment or deprivation.'

Individual Activity

Write the answers to the following questions.

1. Where are teenagers most likely to encounter violent situations?
    _____
    _____

2. What factors could increase the likelihood of teenagers engaging in violent behaviour?
    _____
    _____

3. What sort of acts can violent behaviour include?
    _____
    _____

4. List three acts of violence that can have long-term and serious consequences both for the victim and the person who carries out the violent act.
    a) _____
    b) _____
    c) _____

Class Activity

Discuss your answers with the rest of the class and then consider the following questions.

1. Is violence a problem in your school or community?
2. How does hearing about or witnessing violent acts make you feel?

Using the picture as a prompt, write down a list of strategies to help a teenager avoid becoming involved in a potentially violent situation.

Tips for avoiding violent situations

Learning *Keepsake*

Three things I have learned about violent situations are:

1. _____
2. _____
3. _____

As a result of what I have learned about violent situations, I will:

_____
_____
_____

_____ has shared this Learning Keepsake with me _____
Name of student   Parent's/guardian's signature

Topic Review

Date / /

In this topic I learned about

_____

This topic is useful to me in my life because

_____

_____

In this topic I liked

_____

_____

In this topic I did not like

_____

_____

I would like to find out more about

_____

_____

Key Skills I have used in this topic are:

- ☐ Managing myself
- ☐ Staying well
- ☐ Communicating
- ☐ Being creative
- ☐ Working with others
- ☐ Managing information and thinking

*Are you up for the challenge?

Design a Healthy Living guide for teenagers. Include tips for healthy eating, staying active, relaxation, hygiene and staying safe.

Having a Friend, Being a Friend

● Lesson 16 Boyfriends and Girlfriends

LESSON 16
Boyfriends and Girlfriends

At the end of this lesson . . .

. . . you will have explored the impact of gender roles on friendships

. . . and you will recognise the value of having friendships with people of both sexes.

Key Words
- Gender roles
- Stereotyping

 # Keyskill
- Working with Others

Friendship is very important in all our lives. When we are with our friends we can have fun, we can talk about our lives and we can get support.

It is healthy to have friendships with people of both sexes. Even though we might think that certain qualities belong more to boys and vice versa, it is important not to hold inaccurate stereotypical views.

 Group Activity

Sugar and Spice

What are little boys made of?
What are little boys made of?
Slugs and snails
And puppy-dogs' tails,
That's what little boys are made of.

What are little girls made of?
What are little girls made of?
Sugar and spice
And all things nice,
That's what little girls are made of.

Fill in the table below with three qualities you like about the opposite gender and three qualities you dislike about the opposite gender, e.g. girls are understanding, boys are easy-going; girls are always talking about their feelings, boys cannot be serious about anything.

Remember, when writing your suggestions focus on things that people can change, not on things they cannot change, such as physical characteristics. For what you want to stay the same, think about why you like being friends with people of the opposite gender.

BOY ☐   GIRL ☐ (please tick one)

Like	Dislike
1.	
2.	
3.	

Fill in the table below with three things you like about having friendships with people of the same gender as you, and three things you dislike about having friendships with the same gender.

BOY ☐   **GIRL** ☐ (please tick one)

Like	Dislike
1.	
2.	
3.	

Class Activity

Answer the following questions:

1. What surprised you about what girls say about boys as friends?

2. What surprised you about what boys say about girls as friends?

3. Do you think it is as important to have friends who are the same sex as it is to have friends who are of the opposite sex? Give reasons for your view.

Group Activity

Boys are good friends because . . .

Girls are good friends because . . .

Class Activity

Now discuss your answers with the class.

Individual Activity

Below is a list of qualities that are important in friendships.
Identify which qualities are distinctively male, distinctively female or both by putting a tick in the correct column. Add any qualities you feel have been omitted.

Quality	Male	Female	Both
Good listener			
Up for a laugh			
Loyal			
Funny			
Trustworthy			
Confident			
Easy-going			
Understanding			
Generous			
Honest			
Good-humoured			

Referring to the table, decide on the friendship quality you would most like to develop. It does not have to be a quality that is stereotypically from your gender. Say why you would like to develop this quality.

_____

_____

A quality I would like to develop is:

_____

_____

Why I choose this quality is:

_____

_____

Learning *Keepsake*

Three things I have learned about friendship are:

1. _____
2. _____
3. _____

As a result of what I have learned about friendship, I will:

_____
_____
_____

_____ has shared this Learning Keepsake with me _____

Name of student   Parent's/guardian's signature

Topic Review

Date / /

In this topic I learned about

_____

This topic is useful to me in my life because

_____

_____

In this topic I liked

_____

_____

In this topic I did not like

_____

_____

I would like to find out more about

_____

_____

Key Skills I have used in this topic are:

☐ Managing myself

☐ Staying well

☐ Communicating

☐ Being creative

☐ Working with others

☐ Managing information and thinking

*Are you up for the challenge?

Create a class poster which shows ways you can support someone of the same gender and the opposite gender.

TOPIC 6

Positive Mental Health

LESSON 17

Body Image

Key Words
- Body image
- Celebrities

 # Keyskill
- Staying Well

Self-esteem and body image

Self-esteem is how a person feels about themselves. If you have positive self-esteem, you can accept the way you are.

Body image is how a person feels about their physical appearance. If you have a positive body image, you like and accept the way you are. A person's body image is strongly linked to their self-esteem. Having a good body image does not mean you are full of yourself – it simply means you're comfortable in your own skin. Your body image is influenced by many factors. Some influences are negative and some are positive.

Group Activity

What impact do you think the factors below would have on the body image of someone your age? Give reasons for your answers in the spaces provided.

Influences	Boost body image (likely to make young people happy about their body)	Damage body image (likely to make young people unhappy about their body)
Television		
Celebrities		
Magazines		
Parents		
Friends/classmates		
Teachers		
Advertising		
Other influences		

Class Activity

1. Was there agreement in the group about which were positive and which were negative influences on body image?
2. Are the influences different for boys and girls?
3. Were there any influences that are both positive and negative influences on body image?

Individual Activity

From the list above, identify one factor that has a positive influence on your body image and a factor that has a negative impact on your body image. Give reasons for your answer.

Positive	Negative
Factor: _____ Reason:	Factor: _____ Reason:

1. How easy was it for you to identify the influences on your body image?
   _____
   _____

2. Why you think there are pressures on young people to look a certain way?
   _____
   _____

3. Has your body image changed in the last few years?
   _____
   _____

Achieving and maintaining a positive body image: some tips

1. Remember that it is normal and healthy for young people to come in all shapes and sizes.
2. Try to stay physically fit and eat a healthy diet.
3. Wear clothes that complement your good points.
4. Remember that many of the images of models and celebrities that appear in magazines and on television have been airbrushed and/or digitally enhanced.

Weblink

Watch 'Dove: Evolution of a Model' on youtube.

5. Concentrate on the good things about yourself. Write a list of positive things about yourself and add to it often.
6. Spend time with people who are positive and supportive and make you feel good about yourself.
7. Be media aware. Every time an advertisement tries to sell you a diet or a beauty product it is simply aimed at increasing sales. Just because the advertisers claim that these products will enhance you does not mean that they will.

Three steps to being happy with me

In the first box, write down one thing you can to improve your self-esteem.
In the second box, write down two people who make you feel good about yourself.
In the third box, write three things you like about yourself.

1
2
3

Learning *Keepsake*

Three things I have learned about body image are:

1. _____
2. _____
3. _____

As a result of what I have learned about having a positive body image, I will:

_____
_____
_____

_____ has shared this Learning Keepsake with me _____
Name of student   Parent's/guardian's signature

LESSON 18

Where am I Now?

At the end of this lesson . . .

. . . you will have reviewed the adolescent stages of human growth and development.

Key Words
- Adolescent

 # Keyskill
- Managing Myself

Adolescence

Human development can be roughly divided into three stages: childhood; adolescence; and adulthood. Throughout life people must experience and adapt to many different changes and challenges.

Adolescence is generally regarded as a time of great change in a person's life. Fill in the table below, compare the way you were at nine years of age to how you are now.

Individual Activity

	Nine years old	Teenager
Things you like to do		
Relationships with parents		
Your friendships		
Your interest in the opposite sex		
How you think about your appearance		
How you feel about your own personality		
Your feelings and moods		
Your freedom to do things on your own		
Responsibilities at home		
Do you compare yourself with others, including friends and celebrities		
Your interest in clothes		
Your attitude to school		

1. Were you surprised by any of the changes that have occurred over the last number of years?

_____

2. Do you think your answers will change again in ten years' time? Why?

_____

_____

3. Which changes have had the biggest effect on your life?

_____
_____
_____
_____

4. Do you think that the changes you have experienced are similar to or different from the changes other people your age have experienced?

_____
_____

The development of adolescents

Throughout adolescence, young people continue to develop and change. Many of these changes are not visible in the same way as the changes that come with puberty. However, these changes are very important as a young person continues to grow towards adulthood and it is important for young people to be aware of them.

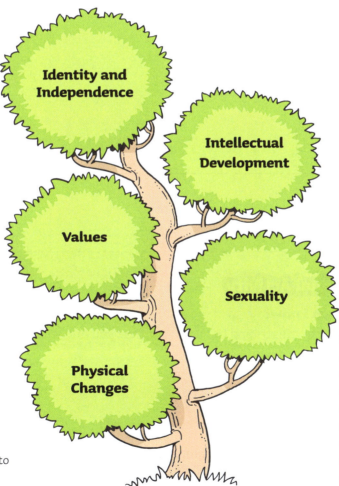

Identity and Independence
Teenagers like to make their own decisions and do not like too much interference from parents.

Adolescents are more concerned with their appearance and body image. Young people can become more reflective and may write music, poetry or keep a diary to process their emotions.

Values
Adolescents no longer accept other people's values without question.

Physical Changes
By this stage many of the changes of puberty may have occurred; however, boys and girls will continue to grow in height and boys may continue to become physically stronger.

Intellectual Development
Adolescents can become more worried and even somewhat anxious about performance at school. The extra energy and enthusiasm that often accompanies adolescence is often displayed in extra efforts with school work and hobbies.

Sexuality
Adolescents are more concerned about being considered attractive by the opposite sex.
Some adolescents may experience confusion and concern about their own sexuality.

Class Activity

Next to each area of development, write down the main challenges and benefits associated with that area for you as a teenager.

Area of development/growth	Challenges for me as a teenager	Benefits for me as a teenager
Identity and independence	E.g. I want to dress a certain way	E.g. I have more independence and freedom
Intellectual development		
Values		
Sexuality		
Physical changes		

Individual Activity

Where am I now?

Write a poem describing the teenager that you are. It doesn't have to rhyme. Include:

- your first name
- four adjectives that describe you
- four things you enjoy doing
- three things you feel
- three things you need
- names of people who support you
- three things that cause you to worry
- three things that have changed for you since you were nine
- three things you hope to achieve in the future

Learning *Keepsake*

Three things I have learned about adolescence are:

1. _____
2. _____
3. _____

As a result of what I have learned about being an adolescent, I will:

_____
_____
_____

_____ has shared this Learning Keepsake with me _____
Name of student   Parent's/guardian's signature

Topic Review

Date / /

In this topic I learned about
_____

This topic is useful to me in my life because
_____
_____

In this topic I liked
_____
_____

In this topic I did not like
_____
_____

I would like to find out more about
_____
_____
_____

Key Skills I have used in this topic are:

☐ Managing myself   ☐ Being creative
☐ Staying well   ☐ Working with others
☐ Communicating   ☐ Managing information and thinking

*Are you up for the challenge?
Using surveys, interviews or other ways to find out about pressures
young people in your school experience to look a certain way.

The Relationship Spectrum

● Lesson 19 Relationships: What's Important?

LESSON 19

Relationships: What's Important?

At the end of this lesson . . .
. . . you will have identified the qualities that are most important to you in a relationship.

Key Words
- Qualities

 # Keyskill
- Working with Others

It is important to know the qualities that are most important to you in a relationship. This will help you to make a good decision when choosing a boyfriend or girlfriend.

 Individual Activity

Look at the qualities associated with each person in the illustrations below. Add any qualities that are not included but that you consider important.

Good looks   Money   Fun   Sporty

 Individual Activity

In the diagram write in the top ten qualities for you in a romantic relationship. Number the qualities 1-10 accordingly to how important you think they are i.e. 1 being the most important to you 10 being the least important.

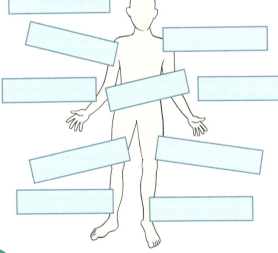

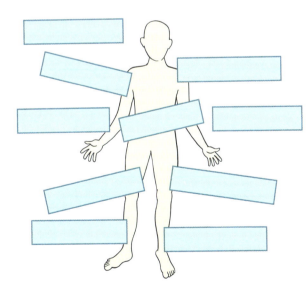

 Group Activity

Compare your top ten qualities with the other people in your group. Choose your groups top ten qualities.

Class Activity

1. Is there anyone whose individual list is very different from their group list?
2. Are there any similarities in the qualities you admire in yourself and those you admire in people you look up to and respect?
3. Why do you think it is important to identify the qualities you are looking for in a relationship?
4. Do you think that boys and girls look for different things in a relationship?
5. Does the type of relationship have an effect on the qualities a person is looking for? Give reasons.
6. What/who do you think influences the qualities a person considers to be important?

Relationships in action

Although it is possible to be in a relationship with somebody who has different qualities from you, if two people in a relationship value different things it may lead to difficulties because:

_____
_____
_____

Difficulties in a relationship can be overcome if:

_____
_____
_____

Difficulties in a relationship may not be resolved if:

_____
_____
_____

The types of relationship we see in the media are not always good role models because:

_____
_____
_____

It is important that the people we are in relationships with have qualities that we value because:

_____
_____
_____

Weblink

Watch the video on 'Attractiveness' from www.b4udecide.ie

Based on what you have learned in this lesson, write down three qualities you would look for in a boyfriend/girlfriend and three things you have to offer.

What I would look for	What I have to offer
1.	1.
2.	2.
3.	3.

Learning *Keepsake*

Three things I have learned about relationships are:

1. _____
2. _____
3. _____

As a result of what I have learned about what is important in a relationship, I will:

_____
_____
_____

_____ has shared this Learning Keepsake with me _____

Name of student   Parent's/guardian's signature

Topic Review

Date / /

In this topic I learned about
_____

This topic is useful to me in my life because
_____
_____

In this topic I liked
_____
_____

In this topic I did not like
_____
_____

I would like to find out more about
_____
_____

Key Skills I have used in this topic are:

☐ Managing myself
☐ Staying well
☐ Communicating
☐ Being creative
☐ Working with others
☐ Managing information and thinking

*Are you up for the challenge?

Using articles, newspaper clippings and magazine create a display showing messages the media give young people about what is important in relationships.

TOPIC 8

Special Relationships

LESSON 20

Healthy vs. Unhealthy Relationships

At the end of this lesson . . .
. . . you will recognise behaviours associated with healthy and unhealthy relationships
. . . you will have explored why people stay in unhealthy relationships
. . . and you will have identified what a person can do if they find themselves in an unhealthy relationship.

Key Words
- Healthy behaviours
- Unhealthy behaviours

Keyskill
- Staying Well

People in healthy relationships experience respect trust and good communication. They enjoy spending time with the other person and they know that each person needs their own space and privacy.

When we are in a romantic relationship it can sometimes be difficult to see that we are not being treated well, especially if we have strong feelings for the other person.

Group Activity

From the list of statements below, decide which statements are characteristic of a healthy relationship and which are characteristic of an unhealthy relationship. When your group has decided, place the statements in the Venn Diagram. If you are not sure about a statement, place it in the middle. You may choose to add extra statements that have not been included.

A My boyfriend sometimes reads my text messages if I leave the room.

B I spend most of my free time with my boyfriend and I don't get to spend much time with my girlfriends any more.

C My girlfriend sometimes puts me down and tells me I'm stupid.

D If something is bothering either of us we always tell the other person.

E My boyfriend and I spend time together but we also make time for our friends.

F I usually keep my feelings to myself – I don't think I can be honest about how I really feel in case he calls it off.

G She says that if I ended this relationship she would do something stupid.

H My boyfriend makes me feel good about myself. He often tells me how good I look.

I I sent a picture by text and he showed it to all his friends.

J My boyfriend thinks it is fun to drive fast in his car and this scares me, but he just laughs when I tell him.

K My boyfriend ignores me at school when he is with his friends. He only ever wants to meet me alone.

L We both have common interests and we decide together what to do in our spare time.

M He hasn't added me as a friend on Facebook and we are going out six months.

N I don't think it is okay if my boyfriend wants to spend time with his friends and not invite me.

O I don't know where I stand with him – I am always worried he is going to call it off.

P We have arguments, but we usually talk them through and we feel better afterwards.

Q I enjoy the time I spend with him. I feel very comfortable in his company and I feel I can say anything to him and I won't be embarrassed.

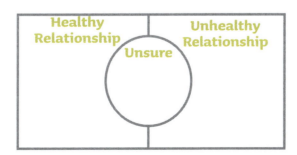

Healthy Relationship | Unhealthy Relationship | Unsure

Weblink

Watch the video on 'Healthy and Unhealthy Relationships' from www.b4udecide.ie.

Denise's story so far . . .

Luke and I were introduced to each other through mutual friends. At first, I was not very interested in Luke but when I got to know him I found myself increasingly attracted to him. We started meeting each other a few weeks later. It was all great at first. We got along very well, we shared common interests and loved spending time together.

As time passes, I have noticed subtle changes in Luke's behaviour. He is becoming more possessive and strange. On two occasions when I left the room, I returned to find him looking at messages on my phone. On a number of occasions Luke passed nasty comments about my family. If we have a disagreement he always blames me. Sometimes when we argue he makes insulting comments about my appearance. Most of the time, when Luke cools off, he apologises to me for his behaviour. He tells me I am the most important person in his life and he is sorry for being such a fool. When I told him I couldn't put up with his behaviour any more, he said he cannot imagine being without me.

The relationship is not always bad and we do have good times, but I make an effort not to do or say anything that might upset him in case he gets angry. On one occasion after a night out with friends at the disco, I argued with Luke because he spoke to his ex-girlfriend for a long time. Luke got so angry with me that he lost his temper and pushed me. He apologised straight away, and it was the first time he has been violent with me. I am considering giving Luke a second chance because I feel I am partly to blame because I provoked him.

Is Denise in a healthy or unhealthy relationship? Give reasons for your answer.

1. Do you think Denise is right to give Luke a second chance in this situation?
2. If you were Denise's friend, what advice would you give her in this situation?
3. Why might she find it difficult to walk away from this relationship?

When to leave

In all types of relationship there will be disagreements and conflicts of interest. These alone do not mean that the relationship is unhealthy. If there is good, open communication, many problems can be worked on and resolved. If there is something in particular a person is unhappy with in their relationship or they want to change, it is important that they communicate how they are feeling with the other person, or with a person they trust. A good friend or family member will help you get an outsider's view on your relationship.

You are not responsible for other people's feelings or actions. Remember, there are some types of behaviour that should never be tolerated. If you are in a relationship that is violent or damaging to your sense of self-worth, you need to get out of it. Talk to someone you trust, an adult or a school counsellor.

In a situation where communication breaks down or a person's personal safety is at risk, the person has no choice but to leave the relationship.

Learning *Keepsake*

Three things I have learned about healthy and unhealthy relationships are:

1. _____
2. _____
3. _____

As a result of what I have learned about relationships, I will:

_____
_____
_____

_____ has shared this Learning Keepsake with me _____
Name of student   Parent's/guardian's signature

LESSON 21

The Three Rs: Respect, Rights and Responsibilities

At the end of this lesson . . .

. . . you will realise that each person in a relationship has rights and responsibilities . . . and you will have improved your assertive communication skills.

Key Words
- Respect
- Rights
- Responsibilities

 # Keyskill
- Working with others
- Communication

What are the three Rs?

The three Rs form the basic structure for forming good relationships. So what does each stand for?

- **Rights**: The way each person deserves to be treated by others. Every young person has the right to be safe and healthy in a relationship. They have the right to make decisions based on their own personal beliefs about what is right and wrong.
- **Respect**: Young people can show respect for each other by valuing a person's rights and ensuring that they take the needs of the other person into account. How you respect a person's rights is measured by your actions.
- **Responsibilities**: What a person must do to ensure another person's rights are respected.

Individual Activity

Below are different rights people have in a relationship. Write the responsibility that goes with each right.

Right to:
- Respect
- My own opinions
- Express myself
- Make decisions about my body
- Have my own friends
- Loyalty
- Privacy
- Love
- Be treated equally
- Be listened to

Responsibility to:
- Respect the rights of others
-
-
-

-
-
-
-

Class Activity

Discuss your answers with the class.

Individual Activity

Read these entries in Jane's diary. In the columns on page 114, fill in the rights and responsibilities Jane has in each situation.

21 October

Dear Diary,

I don't know what to do. I was watching a DVD over in Michael's house last night when his parents were out. We started to kiss on the couch when Michael asked me to go upstairs in case his parents came back early. Before we could go upstairs his parents came in and Michael walked me home. I am supposed to be going over to his house tonight and I don't know what I will do if he asks me to go upstairs.

31 October

Dear Diary,

I'm so upset because I think it's all off between me and Michael. Mr Higgs the science teacher put me and Jim together to work on the science project. I love science and I am really excited about the project. Mr Higgs thinks we might win a prize for the project and we've stayed back after school a couple of times to work on it. Jim is very good fun and ages ago he asked me to go out with him. Michael heard this and asked me not to work on the project any more, but when I said that the project was very important to me and to Jim, he stormed off and now he won't answer my calls or texts.

1 November

Dear Diary,

My mother will not leave me alone. She doesn't like me hanging around with Lucy and Emily because she says their parents give them too much freedom and that they are too grown up. She always makes up excuses when I ask her to let me go out. I know she doesn't trust me because I caught her reading my diary yesterday. She says that she cannot trust me any more just because I have been late home a few times. It wasn't my fault that we missed our lift home, but she never listens to me. Now she won't let me go out tonight and I really wanted to talk about Michael with Lucy and Emily.

15 November

Dear Diary,

Lucy and Emily are always fighting and this time it's really serious. Lucy says that Emily is always copying everything that she wears and that Emily only likes the new boy in school because Lucy said she liked him first. It is getting really awkward now as both of them want me to take their side in the argument. To make it worse, we are all in the same Home Economics class and our teacher said we have to pick a partner for cookery for the year. Both girls have asked me to be their partner and now I feel sick about going into school.

	Jane's rights	Jane's responsibilities
21 October		
31 October		
1 November		
15 November		

1. Describe another situation in which a young person might have to consider their own rights and responsibilities.

   _____

   _____

2. Do you think any of the people Jane wrote about intended to ignore her rights? Give reasons for your answer.

   _____

   _____

   _____

   _____

3. Do you think Jane intended to ignore the rights of the people she wrote about in her diary? Give reasons for your answer.

   _____

   _____

   _____

   _____

4. Choose one of the situations above and write down the advice you would give to Jane.

   _____

   _____

   _____

   _____

Rights and responsibilities: a summary

1. Everybody has rights.
2. Each right that a person has comes with a responsibility to others.
3. Each person has a right to express and assert their rights and a responsibility to respect the rights of others.
4. All relationships are about balancing rights and responsibilities.

Individual Activity: My Diary

Choose one situation from your own life and write a diary entry describing how you expressed one of your own rights in a responsible manner. Name the right and the corresponding responsibility.

Learning Keepsake

Three things I have learned about respect, rights and responsibilities are:

1. _____
2. _____
3. _____

As a result of what I have learned about the three Rs, I will:

_____
_____
_____

_____ has shared this Learning Keepsake with me _____

Name of student   Parent's/guardian's signature

LESSON 22

Conflict and Breaking Up

At the end of this lesson . . .
. . . you will understand that breaking up is a natural part of growing up
. . . and you will be able to identify the appropriate way to end a relationship.

Key Words
- Breaking up
- Communication
- Conflict

Keyskill
- Communicating

Breaking up is hard to do . . .

Sometimes when a relationship is over it is hard for both people involved. One person may feel bad for hurting or upsetting the other person, while the person who is broken up with may feel devastated that the relationship is over.

On the left-hand side of the heart below, write down some reasons why young people might break up. On the right-hand side, write down how a person might feel when a relationship ends.

Moving on: the right way

Look at the following scenario to see both sides of a break-up story.

Two sides of the story

Lucy's side

Me and Steven have been going out together for the last seven months. I thought everything was going well. At the start he made every effort to meet me. He told me he preferred spending time with me to going out with his friends. I told him a lot of personal things, because I really trust him and I needed someone to talk to. Last month he started to meet me less and less. When I met him he made excuses about having a lot of rugby matches and he also said he had to mind his younger brother sometimes. But worst of all, yesterday at school he ignored me completely. My friends said they saw him with a girl from fifth year on Saturday night. I'm so upset. I want to say something to him but I am afraid he will break up with me if I do. I want to tell him I don't mind if I see him less as long as we can stay together.

Steven's side

I have been going out with Lucy for the last seven months. It was great at the start, but I just don't feel the same when I'm with her. I don't fancy her any more, especially since I kissed Katie the other night. I tried to give Lucy some hints, but she is just not getting it. I feel really sorry for her after what she told me about her family and I don't want to break it off to her face. I'll just avoid her for a while and hopefully she will get the message. I really am busy with rugby at the moment so I can use that as an excuse.

Teacher's Book

Role Play

Write a role play in which Steven breaks up with Lucy in the right way.

While one pair is doing the role play, the rest of the class will fill in the observation sheet below.

Observation sheet

1. How did Steven show that he still cares about Lucy's feelings even though they are breaking up?

   _____

   _____

2. How did Lucy show that she respects Steven's right to finish the relationship?

   _____

   _____

3. What could they have done differently/better?

   _____

   _____

4. Based on the role play, how will Steven and Lucy get on the next time they meet?

   _____

   _____

If someone breaks up with you . . .

It is important to remember:

- It is not the end of the world. Everyone has their heart broken sometime, and they survive.
- It might feel very painful now, but in time it gets easier – you will probably look back and wonder why it upset you so much. You might even laugh.
- The person who broke up with you is not necessarily a bad person. They can't stay with you just because you want them to. If they don't want to stay with you, the best they can do is to be honest and respectful in talking to you about it.
- Be sure to talk to someone who cares – a friend, parent or other adult you trust.

Think about the rights and responsibilities you discussed in the last lesson. Write down some of the dos and don'ts when ending a relationship.

Do:	Don't:

Learning Keepsake

Three things I have learned about breaking up are:

1. _____
2. _____
3. _____

As a result of what I have learned about breaking up, I will:

_____
_____
_____

_____ has shared this Learning Keepsake with me _____

Name of student   Parent's/guardian's signature

Topic Review

Date / /

In this topic I learned about

_____

This topic is useful to me in my life because

_____

_____

In this topic I liked

_____

_____

In this topic I did not like

_____

_____

I would like to find out more about

_____

_____

Key Skills I have used in this topic are:

- ☐ Managing myself
- ☐ Staying well
- ☐ Communicating
- ☐ Being creative
- ☐ Working with others
- ☐ Managing information and thinking

*Are you up for the challenge?

Create a layout of a web page which demonstrates ways in which young people can stay safe and responsible within a relationship and where and how to get support if necessary.

MODULE 9

Sexuality and Sexual Health

LESSON 23

Sexual Orientation

At the end of this lesson . . .

. . . you will have learned about the issues faced by gay, lesbian, transgender and bisexual people . . . and you will be able to identify how it is important to respect and accept all people, whatever their sexual orientation.

Key Words
- Gay
- Lesbian
- Bisexual
- Homophobic
- Coming out
- Diversity

Keyskill
- Staying Safe

Weblink

Watch the video 'Stand Up!—Don't Stand for Homophobic Bullying' on youtube

Some definitions

Match each word or phrase with its explanation below.

Definitions:

1. Someone who is attracted romantically, physically and/or emotionally to both sexes.

2. Someone whose gender differs from the one they were given when they were born. They may identify as male or female, or they may feel that neither label fits them.

3. Describes a person's romantic, emotional or sexual attraction to another person. It is associated with a person's feelings and identity.

4. A person who is attracted to someone of the opposite sex – often referred to as 'straight'.

5. The assumption that that everyone is heterosexual or that opposite sex attractions and relationships are both the norm and superior.

☐ **homophobia**

☐ **heterosexism**

☐ **bisexual**

☐ **sexual**

☐ **orientation**

☐ **homosexual**

☐ **diversity**

☐ **coming out**

☐ **transgender**

☐ **ally**

6. A person who is attracted romantically, emotionally and sexually to someone of the same sex.

7. The process through which an LGBT person accepts their sexual orientation or gender identity as part of their overall identity. It not only refers to the process of self acceptance, but also to the act of sharing your identity with others.

8. Negative feelings, attitudes or beliefs directed at non-heterosexual people. A person can be a victim just because other people think they are gay, lesbian or bisexual, even if they are not.

9. Accepting and respecting the variety of different people in a community.

10. People who do not identify as LGBT but support this community by standing against bullying and harassment.

Individual Activity

Lesbian, gay, and bisexual students are part of every student body and contribute to the life of every school. Yet in many schools their sexual identity is not recognised or they are subjected to harassment and homophobic bullying. Constant exposure to verbal harassment can have serious implications for a young person's psychological well-being, as well as impeding their personal and educational development.

Group Activity

What issues do young LGBT students face in school and society?	In what way does homophobic bullying occur in schools?
What could your school do to ensure that LGBT young people are respected in the school community? (e.g. in SPHE class, anti-bullying policies, the school environment, the school student council)	How could we as individuals agree to behave so that LGBT young people feel safe and welcome?

Did you know?

- 5–10% of our population identify as lesbian, gay or bisexual.
- The average age for a person to become aware of their sexual identity is 12.
- The average age for coming out is 17 for young men and 18 for young women.
- The age of sexual consent for homosexuals and heterosexuals is 17.
- Sexual orientation is not a choice and cannot be changed.
- There are support groups for people struggling with their sexuality.
- The Equality Status Act prohibits the harassment of individuals based on their sexual orientation.
- The support service website for LGBT young people in Ireland is www.belongto.org.

Group Activity

Create some slogans/posters that would help to support young LGBT students in your school. Write your favorite slogan in the box below and say why you like it.

Weblink

www.belongto.org

Learning *Keepsake*

Three things I have learned about sexual orientation and transgender are:

1. _____
2. _____
3. _____

As a result of what I have learned about sexual orientation identity, I will:

_____
_____
_____

_____ has shared this Learning Keepsake with me _____
Name of student   Parent's/guardian's signature

LESSON 24

Sexually Transmitted Infections

At the end of this lesson . . .

. . . you will know what an STI is

. . . you will know how to prevent an STI

. . . and you will know how to seek treatment for an STI.

Key Words
- Sexually transmitted infection

Keyskill
- Staying Well

What are STIs?

Sexually transmitted infections (STIs) are a group of infections which can be passed on during sexual intercourse and/or close sexual contact with a person already infected with an STI. Most STIs are caused by viruses or bacteria.

Symptoms that may indicate an STI include:

- unusual discharge from the vagina or penis
- pain or irritation when urinating
- sores, blisters, lumps, rashes or warts near the genitals
- genital itchiness.

These symptoms can also be caused by something other than an STI. A medical check-up and tests will diagnose the cause.

Some STIs have no noticeable symptoms and there may be no way of knowing whether or not a partner is infected. Despite the lack of visible symptoms, STIs can cause serious illness, infertility and even death; so it is extremely important to diagnose and treat STIs. If symptoms seem to disappear the infection can still remain and the infected person can transmit the disease to others.

Once an STI has been diagnosed, partners need to be treated too so that re-infection doesn't occur. Diagnoses and treatment for STIs can be simple and effective; however, there are no cures for some STIs, so prevention is very important.

 Individual Activity

How much do you already know?

Decide whether the following statements are true or false.

		True	False
1.	You can't get an STI if you have had sex with only one person.	☐	☐
2.	You can get an STI through oral sex.	☐	☐
3.	You can prevent STIs by always wearing clean underwear and washing regularly.	☐	☐
4.	Only people who sleep around get STIs.	☐	☐
5.	Once you have had an STI you cannot get another one.	☐	☐
6.	You can self-diagnose an STI.	☐	☐
7.	Anyone can get an STI.	☐	☐
8.	Condoms help prevent the spread of STIs.	☐	☐
9.	Alcohol and drugs can reduce a persons' ability to make responsible decisions about their sexual behaviour.	☐	☐
10.	You can have more than one STI at the same time.	☐	☐

Some common STIs

Chlamydia	• A bacterial infection • May cause vaginal discharge/burning during urination • Often no symptoms • If not treated, it can lead to infertility • Once treated it can be cured quickly and painlessly
Pelvic inflammatory disease	• Caused by an infection such as chlamydia spreading to other parts of the reproduction organs • Can lead to infertility
Genital warts	• Caused by a virus called human papilloma virus • Infects the skin • Causes warts on the genital area • No cure, but the warts can be removed • Linked to cervical cancer
Genital herpes	• Caused by the virus that causes cold sores • Can be passed on by skin-to-skin contact, kissing and sexual intercourse • Unusual discharge • No treatment, but can be kept under control
Gonorrhoea ('the clap')	• A bacterial infection • Often has no symptoms in women, but can lead to infertility • Usually discharge an be cured by antibiotics
Pubic lice ('crabs')	• Cause itchiness in the infected area • Can be passed on by skin-to-skin contact, shared bedding, towels and clothes • Cured with lotions and shampoos similar to those used for head lice
Hepatitis B	• Caused by a virus • Transmitted by contact with blood, semen, vaginal fluid or saliva • A preventive vaccine is available
HIV (human immunodeficiency virus)	• Attacks the immune system • May lead to AIDS • Treatable with HIV medication
Syphilis	• A bacterial infection passed on through sexual contact • No vaccine • Treatable with penicillin

How to prevent STIs

Circle the correct word or phrase in the sentences below.

The risk of catching an STI can be reduced by:

- Not **having/having** sex as part of a relationship.
- Having sex with only **one partner/with many partners**.
- Having sex with only one partner, who also has **no other sexual partners/many sexual partners**.
- Practising safer sex in all sexual relationships, i.e. **not allowing/allowing** blood, semen or vaginal fluids to be exchanged between partners.
- Using condoms **all the time/sometimes**.
- Both partners having **regular/infrequent** check-ups.

Learning *Keepsake*

Three things I have learned about STIs are:

1. _____
2. _____
3. _____

As a result of what I have learned about STIs, I will:

_____
_____
_____

_____ has shared this Learning Keepsake with me _____

Name of student   Parent/guardian's signature

LESSON 25

HIV/AIDS

At the end of this lesson . . .

. . . you will know what HIV and AIDS mean

. . . you will know how HIV is transmitted and how to reduce the risk of getting HIV

. . . you will be prepared for situations that put you at risk as you grow up

. . . and you will understand the negative effects of misinformation about how HIV is passed on.

Key Words
- Risk
- Human immunodeficiency virus
- Acquired immune deficiency syndrome

 # Keyskill
- Staying safe

The red ribbon is the international symbol for HIV and AIDS awareness. It is worn by millions of people, especially on World AIDS Day.

Did you know?

In Ireland, having unprotected sex or sharing needles with an infected person are the two main ways in which people get HIV.

HIV and AIDS

HIV stands for human immunodeficiency virus. It is a virus that weakens humans' immune systems. Our immune system helps us to fight off sickness and infections by attacking germs that enter the body. HIV cannot be cured.

AIDS (acquired immune deficiency syndrome) is a medical condition which is caused by HIV. A person is said to have AIDS when their immune system is damaged so much that it can no longer fight off infections it normally could. A person with AIDS will also develop specific infections. It could take many years for a person with HIV to develop AIDS, and some people with HIV may never go on to develop AIDS.

Many people are unaware of the ways HIV can and cannot be transmitted. In order to protect ourselves, it is important that we don't believe incorrect information. It is also important not to believe rumours around how HIV is transmitted. Scaremongering can lead to fear, stigma and discrimination for a person living with HIV. The following activity will help you identify behaviour that is risky and behaviour that is not.

Group Activity

For each of the following activities, state whether you think the level of risk of getting HIV is High, Medium, Low or No Risk. When you have made your decision, speak to the person to the left of you about why you made the decision. Now choose the person to the right of you and explain your decisions.

RISK	Risk	No Risk	Unsure
Sharing cutlery	☐	☐	☐
Kissing	☐	☐	☐
Sharing a toilet	☐	☐	☐
Mouth-to-mouth resuscitation	☐	☐	☐
Hugging	☐	☐	☐
Protected sex	☐	☐	☐
Sharing needles	☐	☐	☐
Insect bites	☐	☐	☐
Unprotected sex	☐	☐	☐
Getting a tattoo	☐	☐	☐
Sharing a toothbrush	☐	☐	☐
Sharing a swimming pool	☐	☐	☐
Breastfeeding	☐	☐	☐
Donating blood	☐	☐	☐
The unborn child of a pregnant mother	☐	☐	☐
Being coughed on by someone who is infected with HIV	☐	☐	☐
Helping someone who is bleeding without using gloves	☐	☐	☐

Group Activity

Now create an information pamphlet for young people advising them on how to reduce or eliminate the risk of HIV transmission.

PEP

Post Exposure Prophylaxis (PEP) is emergency treatment available to people if they have had a recent exposure to HIV.

Post = after
Exposure = a situation where HIV has a chance to get into someone's blood stream
Prophylaxis = a treatment to stop an infection happening

The medication works by preventing HIV establishing itself in the bloodstream.

Learning *Keepsake*

Three things I have learned about HIV/AIDS are:

1. _____
2. _____
3. _____

As a result of what I have learned about HIV/AIDS, I will:

_____
_____
_____

_____ has shared this Learning Keepsake with me _____
Name of student   Parent's/guardian's signature

Topic Review

Date / /

In this topic I learned about

_____

This topic is useful to me in my life because

_____

_____

In this topic I liked

_____

_____

In this topic I did not like

_____

_____

I would like to find out more about

_____

_____

Key Skills I have used in this topic are:

☐ Managing myself

☐ Staying well

☐ Communicating

☐ Being creative

☐ Working with others

☐ Managing information and thinking

*Are you up for the challenge?
Organise a 'Respect for All' week in your school

Dealing with Tough Times

- Lesson 26 Positive and Negative Stress
- Lesson 27 Managing Stress in our Lives

LESSON 26

Positive and Negative Stress

At the end of this lesson . . .

. . . you will have analysed what causes you stress in your life

. . . you will appreciate the place that stress has in your life

. . . and you will understand different levels of stress.

Key Words
- Stress

Keyskill
- Managing myself

What is stress?

Stress is your body's physical and emotional reaction to circumstances that frighten, irritate, confuse, endanger or excite you. Stress is necessary in life and a certain amount of stress is essential in order to complete tasks and achieve results. However, too much stress is bad for your health. In other words, stress can be positive or negative.

It is important to identify the causes of stress in your life and to understand the different levels of stress that you feel.

The list of stressful situations below contains both positive and negative types of stress. Go through the list and tick off each event that has happened to you in the last year. Decide whether you experienced positive or negative stress. Add any other sources of stress you have experienced.

Event	Did you experience this?	Positive stress?	Negative stress?
Doing something I was not comfortable with because of peer pressure			
Making new friends			
Being accepted by the people in my class			
Falling out with a friend			
Wearing the right clothes			
Performing in the school concert			
Death of a close relation or friend			
Change in family income			
Trying hard but still failing			
Parents giving me too many jobs and responsibilities			
Changing schools			
A threat from a bully			
Preparing for a test			
Getting ready to go to a party			
Not being allowed to go on nights out			
Divorce or separation of parents			
Having trouble with a teacher			
Having an injury or an illness			
Going on holidays			
Competing in the final of a sporting event			

Class Activity

1. How many sources of positive stress are in your life?
2. How many sources of negative stress are in your life?
3. Did anything about this list surprise you?

Stress overload

Our ability to perform increases up to a certain level of stress. There is a point at which we have just enough pressure to perform to the maximum of our ability. Anything more than that level can make us stressed out. When this happens we are experiencing what is called stress overload. Think of the hurler who becomes overwhelmed on All Ireland day or the student who goes blank during an exam. The table below shows the effects of stress on performance.

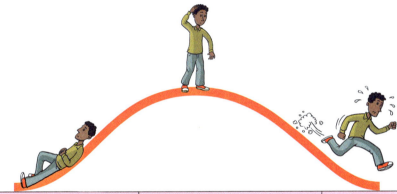

Too little stress	Enough stress	Too much stress
• Too little pressure • Too little challenge • You are bored or lacking in motivation • You are too laid-back • You find it difficult to rise to challenges and reach our goals • You do not have enough pressure to get things done, so other things take priority • You are under-stimulated • You do not perform at our best	• A healthy level of stress • We are alert, energetic and enthusiastic • We are motivated to achieve our goals • At this level of stress we perform at our best • A target or a deadline spurs you on	• We feel unable to cope with the pressure • We feel overwhelmed, anxious, demotivated • We have difficulty in concentrating • We can't meet daily challenges • We do not perform at our best

Imagine these two scenarios and write into the graphs what you think might happen if the person was experiencing too little stress, enough stress and too much stress.

1. Acting in the school play.

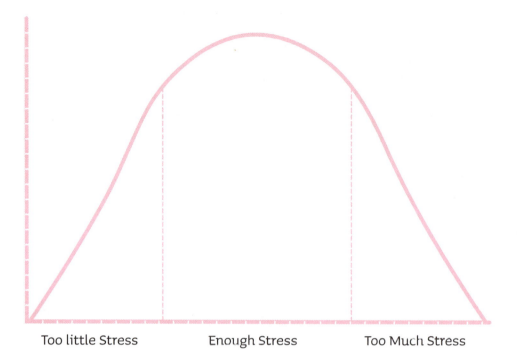

Too little Stress   Enough Stress   Too Much Stress

2. Preparing for an exam.

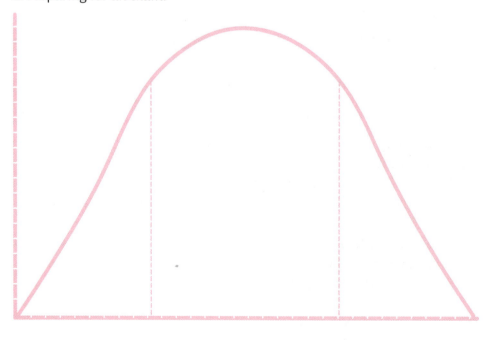

Weblink
www.reachout.com

Learning *Keepsake*

Three things I have learned about stress are:

1. _____
2. _____
3. _____

As a result of what I have learned about stress, I will:

_____
_____

_____ has shared this Learning Keepsake with me _____

Name of student   Parent's/guardian's signature

LESSON 27

Managing Stress in Our Lives

At the end of this lesson . . .

. . . you will have identified the signs of stress

. . . you will know the symptoms of too much stress

. . . and you will have further developed the skills to help you manage stress in your life.

Key Words
- Symptoms
- Behaviour
- Physical effects

Keyskill
- Staying Well
- Managing Myself

In the previous lesson you learned about what causes us stress and the effects of stress on our performance in different situations. You cannot avoid all stress in your life, but you can learn to manage your stress levels. In order to successfully manage stress, it is important to be able to identify what is causing you stress. It is also essential to listen to what your body is telling you and how it is feeling.

When I am stressed . . .

When you feel under a lot of stress and pressure, what happens to you physically? Put a tick beside those that happen often, and a cross beside those that happen only sometimes.

Headaches ☐

Dizziness ☐

Loss of appetite ☐

Heart beats faster ☐

Stomach upset or nausea ☐

Diarrhoea ☐

Tingling fingers and feet ☐

Face feels hot, flushed ☐

Dry mouth or throat ☐

Grind teeth ☐

Neck and shoulders tighten up or ache ☐

Back tightens up or aches ☐

Heartburn ☐

Legs get shaky or tighten up ☐

Breathing fast ☐

Tapping fingers ☐

Knees knocking ☐

Class Activity

1. Were you surprised that these are all symptoms of stress?
2. Are there any other symptoms that could be added?
3. How do you cope with your symptoms of stress?

Where does stress come from?

Thousands of years ago, stress was essential for survival. Our ancestors were often in danger of attack from wild animals, such as wolves and bears. The stress response allowed them to respond to the threat of attack by preparing them for 'fight or flight'. Today this fight-or-flight response works well in situations like running away from a vicious dog.

However, most of the threats in today's world are much less obvious and sometimes our stress response kicks in during exams, conflicts with parents and in relationships with friends. In these situations, neither fight nor flight is an appropriate response, but our body still acts in the same supercharged way.

All of these symptoms are normal responses to stressful situations:

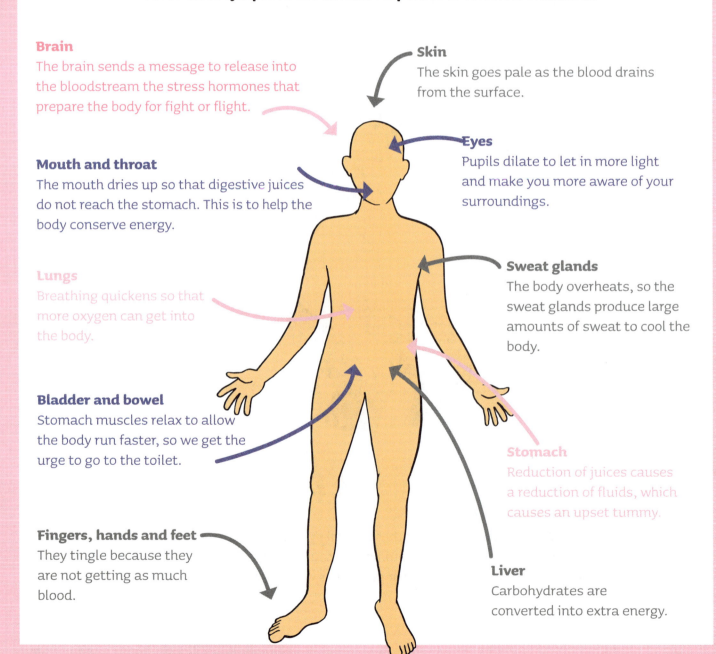

Brain
The brain sends a message to release into the bloodstream the stress hormones that prepare the body for fight or flight.

Mouth and throat
The mouth dries up so that digestive juices do not reach the stomach. This is to help the body conserve energy.

Lungs
Breathing quickens so that more oxygen can get into the body.

Bladder and bowel
Stomach muscles relax to allow the body run faster, so we get the urge to go to the toilet.

Fingers, hands and feet
They tingle because they are not getting as much blood.

Skin
The skin goes pale as the blood drains from the surface.

Eyes
Pupils dilate to let in more light and make you more aware of your surroundings.

Sweat glands
The body overheats, so the sweat glands produce large amounts of sweat to cool the body.

Stomach
Reduction of juices causes a reduction of fluids, which causes an upset tummy.

Liver
Carbohydrates are converted into extra energy.

Class Activity

Discuss with the class any of the signs you recognise.
Are there any signs not included?

It is important to recognise the symptoms of stress early as the effects of stress can be harmful if they go on for too long.

Stress does not just affect us physically; it also affects our thoughts, feelings and behaviours. Here are some common signs and symptoms of too much stress in our lives. Put a tick beside those you often experience and a cross beside those you rarely experience. Add in any other symptoms you have experienced.

Feelings

Irritability ☐
Hopelessness ☐
Anger ☐
Impatience ☐
Being in a 'bad mood' ☐
Edginess or feeling keyed up ☐

Thoughts

'I can't see an end to this' ☐
'I can't do this' ☐
'My problems are huge' ☐
'I'm useless' ☐
'I'm bored' ☐

Behaviour

Crying excessively ☐

Nail biting ☐
Avoiding contact with other people ☐
Using illegal drugs ☐
Overeating ☐
Losing your temper ☐
Becoming accident-prone ☐

We cannot eliminate or avoid all stressful situations in our lives, but we can learn to control our reaction to stress. How we think and behave in certain events can determine how stressful the situation will become. When we are stressed it is very important to stay in control and think positively.

Instead of thinking negatively . . .   . . . think positively

I've got so much to do I'll never get it all done.

I have a lot to do, but if I take one thing at a time I will get it done.

Individual Activity

Now that you can recognise the signs of stress, it is important to look at ways of managing your stress and keeping stress levels at a healthy level.

Common stress controls

- Talk to someone you trust about your concerns.
- Replace negative thoughts with more positive thoughts.
- Be active, run, play a sport, go for a walk or join a dancing group.
- Accept what you cannot change.
- Plan ahead. Make lists. Do one task at a time.
- Learn to say no to people: remember, you can't please everybody. Things I already do to control my stress:

_____
_____
_____
_____
_____
_____
_____
_____

Three other stress controls I could use:

1. _____
_____

2. _____
_____

3. _____
_____

Someone I would call on to support me in a stressful situation is

_____

Weblink

www.letsomeoneknow.ie

Learning *Keepsake*

Three things I have learned about stress are:

1. ....
2. ....
3. ....

As a result of what I have learned about stress, I will:

....
....

.... has shared this Learning Keepsake with me ....

Name of student   Parent's/guardian's signature

Topic Review

Date   /   /

In this topic I learned about

_____

This topic is useful to me in my life because

_____

_____

In this topic I liked

_____

_____

In this topic I did not like

_____

_____

I would like to find out more about

_____

_____

Key Skills I have used in this topic are:

- ☐ Managing myself
- ☐ Staying well
- ☐ Communicating
- ☐ Being creative
- ☐ Working with others
- ☐ Managing information and thinking

*Are you up for the challenge?

Design a resource highlighting ways in which young people can look after their mental health.

Mental Health/ Mental Ill Health

LESSON 28

Feelings and Moods

At the end of this lesson . . .
. . . you will be aware of the feelings and moods that occur in adolescence
. . . and you will be better able to express your feelings.

Key Words
- Overwhelmed

Keyskill
- Staying Well

As a teenager you will experience many new feelings and thoughts. There are times when you feel up and times when you feel down. You might feel confident, relaxed and happy most of the time, but sometimes you might feel sad, confused or worried. These highs and lows are normal. As well as all the changes going on in your body, other parts of your life are changing too. You have a lot more responsibilities now than when you were a child and you are still developing the skills and knowledge to cope with these added pressures. Your relationships with your family and friends are also changing and at times these relationships may be quite frustrating.

Remember: only talk about what you are comfortable with. If an issue arises that upsets you, talk privately to your teacher or to another trusted adult.

The things that make me feel good are:

Spending time with friends

Being praised

Things that make me feel unpleasant, worried, sad, embarrassed etc. are:

How easy was it to think of things that make you feel good?

_____

List some of the pleasant feelings you get from these things.

_____

_____

_____

How easy was it to think of the things that made you feel bad?

_____

List some of the unpleasant feelings you get from these things.

_____

_____

_____

Would other people have known how you were feeling? How would they have known?

_____

_____

Who was affected by how you were feeling?

_____

_____

Sometimes our feelings are so strong that we can be overwhelmed by them. At times, you might find it difficult to cope with how you are feeling. It is important to recognise your feelings, to understand why you have those feelings, and to have healthy ways for dealing with them.

If your friend was feeling the same way, what advice would you have given them?

_____

_____

If you felt like this again, what would you do?

_____

_____

Dealing with difficult situations

We all experience times of stress, trauma, rejection or failure. These are part of life. When things go wrong and we are feeling down, there are many things we can do to help us cope. Different things work for different people. There are also unhelpful things we can do that make it more difficult to deal with the situation, for example drinking or smoking too much.

Look at the coping strategies below. Put an X through strategies you should avoid and a circle around those you should use.

Write how you are feeling in a diary/journal

Do absorbing activities (e.g. crosswords, puzzles) that take your mind off your worries

Blame yourself

Ignore the problem and hope it will go away

Use humour

Overeat

Contact a help agency

Pretend nothing is wrong

Meditate

Talk to someone about how you're feeling

Keep busy – try to keep your mind off your worries

Think positive thoughts

Think of the worst-case scenario

Talk to friends or family members about your problems or worries

Close yourself off and avoid people

Use negative self-talk

Sit down and try to come up with a plan to tackle the problem

Foresee the best outcome

Abuse substances such as alcohol or cigarettes

Don't eat enough

Get angry and lose your temper

Worry excessively

Take time out and come back to it later

Play a game or take exercise

Weblink
www.headsup.ie

It is very important to seek help or talk to someone you trust if you are feeling down or worried. 'A problem shared is a problem halved.'

Why do you think some people are reluctant to tell others if they are feeling down or sad?

_____

_____

_____

_____

What are the benefits of talking to someone about our problems?

_____

_____

_____

_____

Remember: if a friend or a family member tells you they are feeling depressed, are self-harming or are feeling suicidal, you **must** tell someone who can help. Do not keep this information to yourself.

Learning *Keepsake*

Three things I have learned about moods and feelings are:

1. _____
2. _____
3. _____

As a result of what I have learned about moods and feelings, I will:
_____
_____
_____

_____ has shared this Learning Keepsake with me _____

Name of student   Parent's/guardian's signature

LESSON 29

Depression

At the end of this lesson . . .

. . . you will have an awareness of the symptoms of depression

. . . and you will have identified ways of helping someone with depression.

Key Words
- Upset
- Chemical changes
- Stress
- Hormones

Keyskill
- Staying Well

Depression

John is 15 and he has been feeling down for the last three weeks. John used to love playing many different sports but has now lost all interest. He has also been refusing to go to school because he just isn't up to talking to people. He feels that everyone will know that he is down and they will think that he is strange. He doesn't think anyone would want to be in his company because he is feeling so miserable and he has not contacted any of his friends in two weeks.

John is finding it hard to concentrate or focus on any tasks and whenever his mother gives him a job it ends in an argument because he just doesn't have the energy to do it. His mother thinks that he is being awkward.

John wants to be happy and he feels bad for feeling down and upsetting others. He feels useless.

Tick the box beside each statement you most agree with.

John is:
• Just going through a bad patch ☐
• Depressed ☐
• A moody teenager ☐

John should:
• Snap out of it ☐
• Go out and get drunk ☐
• Go to the doctor to get help ☐

John could:
• See a doctor ☐
• Talk to someone he trusts ☐
• Call a helpline ☐
• Just let up and get on with things ☐

If John doesn't do something, he might:
• Just snap out of it anyway ☐
• Lose all his friends ☐
• Get worse ☐

People who are depressed are:
• Full of self-pity ☐
• Losers ☐
• Just like me ☐
• Unwell ☐

If my friend was depressed I could:
• Try to cheer them up by telling jokes ☐
• Tell them I'm there for them ☐
• Encourage them to talk to someone ☐
• Tell them to 'get over it' and move on ☐

Class Activity

Compare your answers with the rest of the class.

Weblink

www.leanonme.ie

What is depression?

As we discussed in the last lesson, there are times when we feel sad and down. Sometimes this is because of a setback or disappointment. Usually these feelings don't last and we are back to normal in a few days or hours.

Some people, however, can find it difficult to escape this low mood. They can experience long-lasting feelings of sadness and hopelessness to a point where they find it difficult to take part in day-to-day activities. If this is the case the person may be suffering from a medical condition known as clinical depression. Clinical depression is a treatable condition. It can affect people in different ways, and not everyone with depression will have the same symptoms, but it is important that a person seeks professional help if they have symptoms for more than two weeks or if they have thoughts of self-harm or suicide.

Symptoms of depression

The acronym FESTIVAL helps describe how depression can affect us.

Feeling: depressed, sad, anxious or bored.

Energy: low energy, feeling tired or fatigued.

Sleep: under or over sleeping, frequent waking during the night.

Thinking: slow or negative thinking or poor concentration.

Interest: loss of interest in school, hobbies, food, family.

Value: low self-esteem; feeling worthless.

Aches: physical aches and pains with no physical basis e.g. chest/head/tummy pain associated with anxiety or stress.

Living: loss of interest in living, thinking about death or suicide.

Source: adapted from www.aware.ie.

Causes of depression

Depression can affect anyone and in some people it can happen suddenly and for no reason. However, there are some factors which make some people more at risk to depression.

1. Genes do appear to play a role in depression, but just because one family member is affected by depression does not mean that their relations will be too.
2. Chemical changes in the brain can lead to symptoms of depression.
3. Hormones can also play a part. For example, if a person has experienced too much negative stress they might have too much of the 'stress hormone' cortisol in their body, which can cause depression.
4. Social and environmental factors such as:

- poverty
- health issues
- money worries
- loneliness
- unemployment
- bereavement
- divorce/separation
- bullying
- trauma
- alcohol and drug abuse.

How you can help

If you suspect that a friend is affected by depression, you can be supportive by following this advice.

Do	Don't
Take them seriously	Make a joke of their situation
Tell them you are there for them	Tell them to pull themselves together
Advise them to seek professional help	Tell them you are just as depressed as they are
Acknowledge their strengths in a specific way, e.g. 'You had two very good days last week'	Tell them to stop feeling sorry for themselves
Support them in healthy lifestyle choices, e.g. eating, exercising and relaxing	Tell them to look at all the worse things that are happening to other people
Offer your company and time	Blame them – it is not their fault
Remind them you can take care of yourself, they don't need to worry about upsetting you	Avoid them

Pair Activity

Imagine your friend has depression. Role play in pairs what you would say to them.

Learning *Keepsake*

Three things I have learned about depression are:

1. _____
2. _____
3. _____

As a result of what I have learned about depression, I will:

_____

_____

_____

_____ has shared this Learning Keepsake with me _____

Name of student   Parent's/guardian's signature

LESSON 30

Help Agencies

At the end of this lesson . . .
. . . you will know about some help agencies
. . . and you will how to contact them.

Key Words
- Support network
- Community

 # Keyskill
- Staying Well

Match the help agencies logo to the service they provide.

1. Offers advice and support to those who have been affected by alcohol problems.

2. Offers support to people who are affected by eating disorders.

3. Offers support to people with depression.

4. Provides support and information for those affected by an unplanned pregnancy.

5. Provides 24/7 support for people who are experiencing emotional difficulty.

6. Telephone and online services for children who need someone to listen.

7. An automated 24-hour service that offers a text-based support service for young people experiencing difficulty in their daily lives.

8. Offers support to young people who are grieving a death, separation or other painful transition in life.

9. Supports lesbian, gay, bisexual and transgender young people in Ireland.

10. Dedicated to tackling poverty in all its forms.

Who can I contact for help?

Family Troubles

Seamus's parents recently separated. Seamus's dad has left the family home. Seamus is really angry with his dad and won't speak to him. Seamus has also lost interest in his friends and his hobbies.

How do you think Seamus feels about asking for help?

_____

_____

Who could Seamus turn to for support?

_____

What sort of support could they give him?

_____

From the help agencies you have looked at, which would be the best one for Seamus to contact? Give reasons for your answer.

_____

_____

_____

Where am I?

Jane is in an all-girls' secondary school. She is in third year. Recently she has been confused about her sexuality: she has feelings towards one of the girls in her class.

How do you think Jane feels about asking for support?

_____

Who could Jane turn to for support?

_____

What sort of support could they give her?

_____

From the help agencies you have looked at, which would be the best one for Jane to contact? Give reasons for your answer.

_____

_____

_____

Extra Stress

Joe is studying for his Junior Cycle exams. Despite working really hard, his class test results are not improving. His parents think he is not working as hard as he should be. His friends seem to get good grades with a fraction of the work he puts in. Joe feels under a lot of pressure.

How do you think Joe feels about asking for support?

_____

Who could Joe turn to for support?

_____

What sort of support could they give him?

_____

From the help agencies you have looked at, which would be the best one for Joe to contact? Give reasons for your answer.

_____

_____

_____

Contacting help agencies

Most help agencies have a website, a helpline or an email address.
Before contacting an agency, be clear about what you want to say – writing it down might help you.

Contact addresses and telephone numbers are available from:
- school guidance counsellors
- the telephone directory
- your GP
- the internet.

When you contact the organisation you will:
- speak to a trained counsellor who will listen to what you have to say
- be guaranteed confidentiality and anonymity
- be free to answer or not answer any questions that the counsellor may ask you – if you are not comfortable about answering a question, you can decide not to.

Weblink

www.headsup.ie

Individual Activity

Select a help agency of your choice and design a resource – e.g. a poster, website, PowerPoint presentation or leaflet – to raise awareness in your school about the services the agency provides. Remember to include:

- name of the agency
- contact details
- the service it provides.

Learning *Keepsake*

Three things I have learned about help agencies are:

1. _____
2. _____
3. _____

As a result of what I have learned about help agencies, I will:

_____

_____

_____

_____ has shared this Learning Keepsake with me _____
Name of student   Parent's/guardian's signature

Topic Review

Date / /

In this topic I learned about

_____

This topic is useful to me in my life because

_____

_____

In this topic I liked

_____

_____

In this topic I did not like

_____

_____

I would like to find out more about

_____

_____

Key Skills I have used in this topic are:

☐ Managing myself
☐ Staying well
☐ Communicating
☐ Being creative
☐ Working with others
☐ Managing information and thinking

*Are you up for the challenge?

Research mental health services available to young people in your area and draw up a booklet based on this information.

TOPIC 12

Substance Use

- Lesson 31 Ecstasy, Cocaine and Heroin: The Reality

LESSON 31
Ecstasy, Cocaine and Heroin: the Reality

At the end of this lesson . . .

. . . you will know about the personal and social dangers associated with the use of Ecstasy

. . . and you will know about the personal and social dangers – including addiction – associated with the use of cocaine and heroin.

Key Words
- Abuse
- Addiction

Keyskill
- Staying Safe

 **Group Activity**

The facts

The misuse of Ecstasy, heroin and cocaine can have seriously damaging effects on all areas of a person's life. It is important to know the correct facts about these drugs.

Let's see what you already know. Answer the questions about each drug below.

Question	Ecstasy	Cocaine	Heroin
What does the law say?			
What are its slang names?			
How is it taken?			
What are the risks and dangers of using this drug for drug users			
How might widespread use of this drug harm communities?			

Individual Activity

How difficult or easy did you find this activity?

_____
_____
_____

Which drug did you know most about? Where did you get your information from?

_____
_____
_____

Why do you think it is important to learn about drugs?

_____
_____
_____

Which drug did you know least about? Why do you think this was?

_____
_____
_____

Using the information on these three drugs that your teacher will give you, use a different-coloured pen to fill in anything you did not know already.
Was there anything that surprised you about what you learned?

_____
_____
_____

You have probably seen health warnings on cigarette packets similar to the one in the picture. Design a health warning for Ecstasy, heroin and cocaine in the boxes below.

Heroin

Ecstasy

Cocaine

Weblink

www.drugs.ie

Learning *Keepsake*

Three things I have learned about substance use are:

1. _____
2. _____
3. _____

As a result of what I have learned about substance use, I will:

_____
_____
_____

_____ has shared this Learning Keepsake with me _____

Name of student   Parent's/guardian's signature

Topic Review

Date / /

In this topic I learned about

_____

This topic is useful to me in my life because

_____

_____

In this topic I liked

_____

_____

In this topic I did not like

_____

_____

I would like to find out more about

_____

_____

Key Skills I have used in this topic are:

☐ Managing myself

☐ Staying well

☐ Communicating

☐ Being creative

☐ Working with others

☐ Managing information and thinking

*Are you up for the challenge?

Design a resource outlining where and how to get help for yourself or others for problems associated with substance use.